A Brief Introduction to Judaism

A Brief Introduction to
JUDAISM

Updated and revised by Tim Dowley

General Editor: Christopher Partridge

Fortress Press

Minneapolis

The maps and images on pages 110-126 appear in *Atlas of World Religions*
(Fortress Press, forthcoming).

Cover image: Blue Floral Tile Floor Found in Israel/iStock.com/Linda Johnsonbaugh;
Unwrapped Torah scroll silver/iStock.com/OqIpo
Cover design: Laurie Ingram

Print ISBN: 978-1-5064-5040-7
eBook ISBN: 978-1-5064-5041-4

The paper used in this publication meets the minimum requirements of American
National Standard for Information Sciences — Permanence of Paper for Printed
Library Materials, ANSI Z329.48-1984.

Manufactured in the USA

CONSULTING EDITORS

Contents

PART 1
UNDERSTANDING RELIGION

PART 2
JUDAISM

Contributors

David Arnold: *I am a Jew*

Dr Robert Banks, formerly Home L. Goddard Professor of the Ministry of the Laity, Fuller Theological Seminary, Pasadena, California, USA: *The Covenant*

Dr Fiona Bowie, Honorary Research Fellow, Department of Archaeology and Anthropology, University of Bristol, UK: *The Anthropology of Religion, Ritual and Performance*

Dr Jeremy Carrette, Professor of Religion and Culture, University of Kent, England: *Critical Theory and Religion*

Dr Eric S. Christianson, formerly Senior Lecturer in Biblical Studies, University College Chester, UK: *Judaism: Sacred Writings*

Dr Dan Cohn-Sherbok, Professor Emeritus of Judaism, University of Wales, UK: *Judaism: Beliefs, The Holocaust*

Dr Geoffrey Cowling, formerly Senior Lecturer in History, Macquarie University, New South Wales, Australia: *Judaism: A Historical Overview*

Dr Douglas Davies, Professor in the Study of Religion, Department of Theology and Religion, University of Durham, UK: *Myths and Symbols*

Dr Malcolm Hamilton, Senior Lecturer, Department of Sociology, University of Reading, UK: *The Sociology of Religion*

Dr David Harley, former Principal, All Nations Christian College, Ware, Herts, UK: *Judaism: Family and Society*

Dr Elizabeth Ramsey, Lecturer, Liverpool Hope University College, UK: *Judaism: Worship and Festivals, Judaism in the Modern World*

Dr Elizabeth J. Harris, Senior Lecturer, Comparative Study of Religions, Liverpool Hope University, UK: *Buddhism: Beliefs, Family and Society, Buddhism in the Modern World*

Dr Paul Hedges, Senior Lecturer in Theology and Religious Studies: *Theological Approaches to the Study of Religion*

Magdalen Lambkin, PhD, University of Glasgow, Scotland: Consultant, *Understanding Religion*

Dr Russell T. McCutcheon, Professor of Sociology of Religion, University of Alabama, USA: *What is Religion?*

Dr Christopher Partridge, Professor of Religious Studies, University of Lancaster, UK: *Phenomenology and the Study of Religion, Rapid Fact-finder*

Revd Angela Tilby, Diocesan Canon, Christ Church, Oxford, UK: *Rapid Fact-finder*

Dr Alana Vincent, Lecturer in Jewish Studies, University of Chester, UK: Consultant, *Judaism*

Dr Fraser N. Watts, Starbridge Lecturer in Theology and Natural Science, University of Cambridge, UK: *The Psychology of Religion*

Dr Paul Williams, Emeritus Professor of Indian and Tibetan Philosophy, University of Bristol, UK: *Buddhism: A Historical Overview, Sacred Writings*

Revd Dr Marvin R. Wilson, Harold J. Ockenga Professor of Biblical and Theological Studies, Gordon College, Wenham, MA, USA: *Branches of Judaism*

Revd Dr John-David Yule, Incumbent of the United Benefice of Fen Drayton with Conington, Lolworth, and Swavesey, Cambridge, UK: *Rapid Fact-finder*

List of Maps

List of Time Charts

List of Festival Charts

List of Illustrations

Preface

This volume and five other titles in the *Brief Introductions* series are taken directly from the third edition of *Introduction to World Religions*, edited by Christopher Partridge and revised by Tim Dowley. Additional maps and images are included from *Atlas of World Religions*, edited by Tim Dowley. We recognized that smaller volumes focused on specific religious traditions might be especially helpful for use in corresponding religious studies courses. General readers who are eager to know and understand more about religious beliefs and practices will find this series to be an engaging and accessible way to explore the world's religions—one by one.

Other Books in the Series
A Brief Introduction to Buddhism
A Brief Introduction to Christianity
A Brief Introduction to Hinduism
A Brief Introduction to Islam
A Brief Introduction to Jainism and Sikhism

PART I
UNDERSTANDING RELIGION

SUMMARY

Belief in something that exists beyond or outside our understanding – whether spirits, gods, or simply a particular order to the world – has been present at every stage in the development of human society, and has been a major factor in shaping much of that development. Unsurprisingly, many have devoted themselves to the study of religion, whether to understand a particular set of beliefs, or to explain why humans seem instinctively drawn to religion. While biologists, for example, may seek to understand what purpose religion served in our evolutionary descent, we are concerned here with the beliefs, rituals, and speculation about existence that we – with some reservation – call religion.

The question of what 'religion' actually is is more fraught than might be expected. Problems can arise when we try to define the boundaries between religion and philosophy when speculation about existence is involved, or between religion and politics when moral teaching or social structure are at issue. In particular, once we depart from looking at the traditions of the West, many contend that such apparently obvious distinctions should not be applied automatically.

While there have always been people interested in the religious traditions of others, such 'comparative' approaches are surprisingly new. Theology faculties are among the oldest in European universities, but, while the systematic internal exploration of a religion provides considerable insights, many scholars insisted that the examination of religions more generally should be conducted instead by objective observers. This phenomenological approach was central to the establishment of the study of religion as a discipline in its own right. Others, concerned with the nature of society, or the workings of the human mind, for example, were inevitably drawn to the study of religion to expand their respective areas. More recently, many have attempted to utilise the work of these disparate approaches. In particular, many now suggest that – because no student can ever be entirely objective – theological studies are valuable because of their ability to define a religion in its own terms: by engaging with this alongside other, more detached, approaches, a student may gain a more accurate view of a particular religion.

CHAPTER I

What Is Religion?

Although no one is certain of the word's origins, we know that 'religion' derives from Latin, and that languages influenced by Latin have equivalents to the English word 'religion'. In Germany, the systematic study of religion is known as *Religionswissenschaft*, and in France as *les sciences religieuses*. Although the ancient words to which we trace 'religion' have nothing to do with today's meanings — it may have come from the Latin word that meant to tie something tightly (*religare*) — it is today commonly used to refer to those beliefs, behaviours, and social institutions which have something to do with speculations on any, and all, of the following: the origin, end, and significance of the universe; what happens after death; the existence and wishes of powerful, non-human beings such as spirits, ancestors, angels, demons, and gods; and the manner in which all of this shapes human behaviour.

Because each of these makes reference to an invisible (that is, non-empirical) world that somehow lies outside of, or beyond, human history, the things we name as 'religious' are commonly thought to be opposed to those institutions which we label as 'political'. In the West today we generally operate under the assumption that, whereas religion is a matter of personal belief that can never be settled by rational debate, such things as politics are observable, public, and thus open to rational debate.

THE ESSENCE OF 'RELIGION'

Although this commonsense distinction between private and public, sentiment and action, is itself a historical development — it is around the seventeenth century that we first see evidence that words that once referred to one's behaviour, public standing, and social rank (such as piety and reverence) became sentimentalized as matters of private feeling — today the assumption that religion involves an inner core of belief that is somehow expressed publicly in ritual is so widespread that to question it appears counterintuitive. It is just this assumption that inspires a number of people who, collectively, we could term 'essentialists'. They are 'essentialists' because they maintain that 'religion' names the outward behaviours that are inspired by the inner thing they call 'faith'. Hence, one can imagine someone saying, 'I'm not religious, but I'm spiritual.' Implicit here is the assumption that the institutions associated with religions — hierarchies, regulations, rituals, and so on — are merely secondary and inessential; the important thing is the inner faith, the inner 'essence' of religion. Although the essence of religion — the thing without which someone is thought to be non-religious — is known by various names (faith, belief, the Sacred, the Holy, and so on), essentialists are in general agreement that the essence of religion is real and non-empirical (that is, it cannot itself be seen, heard, touched, and so on); it defies study and must be experienced first-hand.

THE FUNCTION OF 'RELIGION'

Apart from an approach that assumes an inner experience, which underlies religious behaviour, scholars have used the term 'religion' for what they consider to be curious areas of observable human behaviour which require an explanation. Such people form theories to account for why it is people think, for example, that an invisible part of their body, usually called 'the soul', outlives that body; that powerful beings control the universe; and that there is more to existence than what is observable. These theories are largely functionalist; that is, they seek to determine the social, psychological, or political role played by the things we refer to as 'religious'. Such functionalists include historically:

- Karl Marx (1818–83), whose work in political economy understood religion to be a pacifier that deadened oppressed people's sense of pain and alienation, while simultaneously preventing them from doing something about their lot in life, since ultimate responsibility was thought to reside in a being who existed outside history.

Karl Marx (1818–83).

- Émile Durkheim (1858–1917), whose sociology defined religious as sets of beliefs and practices to enable individuals who engaged in them to form a shared, social identity.
- Sigmund Freud (1856–1939), whose psychological studies prompted him to liken religious behaviour to the role that dreams play in helping people to vent antisocial anxieties in a manner that does not threaten their place within the group.

Although these classic approaches are all rather different, each can be understood as *functionalist* insomuch as religion names an institution that has a role to play in helping individuals and communities to reproduce themselves.

THE FAMILY RESEMBLANCE APPROACH

Apart from the *essentialist* way of defining religion (i.e. there is some non-empirical, core feature without which something is not religious) and the *functionalist* (i.e. that religions help to satisfy human needs), there is a third approach: the *family resemblance* definition. Associated with the philosophy of Ludwig Wittgenstein (1889–1951), a family resemblance approach assumes that nothing is defined by merely one essence or function. Rather, just as members of a family more or less share a series of traits, and just as all things we call 'games' more or less share a series of traits — none of which is distributed evenly across all members of those groups we call 'family' or 'games' — so all things — including religion — are defined insomuch as they more or less share a series of delimited traits. Ninian Smart (1927–2001), who identified seven dimensions of religion that are present in religious traditions with varying degrees of emphasis, is perhaps the best known proponent of this view.

'RELIGION' AS CLASSIFIER

Our conclusion is that the word 'religion' likely tells us more about the user of the word (i.e. the classifier) than it does about the thing being classified. For instance, a Freudian psychologist will not conclude that religion functions to oppress the masses, since the Freudian theory precludes coming up with this Marxist conclusion. On the other hand, a scholar who adopts Wittgenstein's approach will sooner or later come up with a case in which something seems to share some traits, but perhaps not enough to count as 'a religion'. If, say, soccer matches satisfy many of the criteria of a religion, what might not also be called religion if soccer is? And what does such a broad usage do to the specificity, and thus utility, of the word 'religion'? As for those who adopt an essentialist approach, it is likely no coincidence that only those institutions with which one agrees are thought to be expressions of some authentic inner experience, sentiment, or emotion, whilst the traditions of others are criticized as being shallow and derivative.

So what is religion? As with any other item in our lexicon, 'religion' is a historical artefact that different social actors use for different purposes: to classify certain parts of their social world in order to celebrate, degrade, or theorize about them. Whatever else it may or may not be, religion is at least an item of rhetoric that group members use to sort out their group identities.

RUSSELL T. MCCUTCHEON

CHAPTER 2

Phenomenology and the Study of Religion

There is a long history of curiosity and scholarship regarding the religions of other people. However, the study of religions is a relative newcomer to academia. Greatly indebted to the impressive work and influence of the German scholar Friedrich Max Müller (1823–1900), the first university professorships were established in the final quarter of the nineteenth century. By the second half of the twentieth century, the study of religion had emerged as an important field of academic enquiry. In a period of history during which the rationalism of the earlier part of the century saw a decline, and in which there was increased interest in particularly non-Christian spirituality, since 1945 there has been a growth in courses in the study of religion offered in academic institutions. Moreover, work done in other disciplines has increasingly converged with the work done by students of religion (see the discussion in this book of 'The Anthropology of Religion', 'The Psychology of Religion', 'The Sociology of Religion', and 'Critical Theory and Religion').

These factors, amongst others, have made it possible for the study of religion in most Western universities to pull away from its traditional place alongside the study of Christian theology and establish itself as an independent field of enquiry. Whereas earlier in the century the study of non-Christian faiths was usually undertaken in faculties of Christian theology, and studied as part of a theology degree, there was a move – particularly in the late 1960s and 1970s, when the term 'religious studies' became common currency – to establish separate departments of religious studies. Whilst in the United States and most of Western Europe religious studies tends to be considered a subject completely distinct from theology, in the United Kingdom it is quite common for universities to offer degree programmes in 'theology and religious studies', and the lines between the two disciplines are not so heavily drawn.

RELIGIONSPHÄNOMENOLOGIE

Phenomenology is distinct from other approaches to the study of religion in that it does not necessarily seek to understand the social nature of religion, it is not concerned to explore the psychological factors involved in religious belief, nor is it

During the Kumbh Mela festival in the holy city of Haridwar the Guru in his decorated chariot is escorted by holy men and pilgrims visiting the River Ganges, India.

especially interested in the historical development of religions. Rather its main concern has been descriptive, the classification of religious phenomena: objects, rituals, teachings, behaviours, and so on.

The term *Religionsphänomenologie* was first used by the Dutch scholar Pierre Daniel Chantepie de la Saussaye (1848–1920) in his work *Lehrbuch der Religions-geschichte* (1887), which simply documented religious phenomena. This might be described as 'descriptive' phenomenology, the aim being to gather information about the various religions and, as botanists might classify plants, identify varieties of particular religious phenomena. This classification of types of religious phenomena, the hallmark of the phenomenological method, can be seen in the works of scholars such as Ninian Smart (1927–2001) and Mircea Eliade (1907–86). Descriptive phenomenology of the late nineteenth and early twentieth centuries tended to lead to accounts of religious phenomena which, to continue with the analogy, read much the same as a botanical handbook. Various species were identified (higher religion, lower religion, prophetic religion, mystical religion, and so on) and particular religious beliefs and practices were then categorized, discussed, and compared.

As the study of religion progressed, phenomenology came to refer to a method which was more complex, and claimed rather more for itself, than Chantepie's mere cataloguing of facts. This later development in the discipline – which was due in part to the inspiration of the philosophy of Edmund Husserl (1859–1938) – recognized how easy it is for prior beliefs and interpretations unconsciously to influence one's thinking. Hence, scholars such as Gerardus van der Leeuw (1890–1950) stressed the need for phenomenological *epoché*: the 'bracketing' or shelving of the question about the ontological or objective status of the religious appearances to consciousness. Thus questions about the objective or independent truth of Kali, Allah, or the Holy Spirit are initially laid aside. The scholar seeks to suspend judgment about the beliefs of those he studies in order to gain greater objectivity and accuracy in understanding. Also central to phenomenology is the need for empathy (*Einfühlung*), which helps towards an understanding of the religion from within. Students of a religion seek to feel their way into the beliefs of others by empathizing with them. Along with this suspension of judgment and empathy, phenomenologists spoke of 'eidetic vision', the capacity of the observer to see beyond the particularities of a religion and to grasp its core essence and meaning. Whilst we often see only what we want, or expect, to see, eidetic vision is the ability to see a phenomenon without such distortions and limitations. Hence, later phenomenologists did not merely catalogue the facts of religious history, but by means of *epoché*, empathy, and eidetic vision sought to understand their meaning for the believer. Although phenomenologists are well aware that there will always be some distance between the believer's understandings of religious facts and those of the scholar, the aim of phenomenology is, as far as possible, to testify only to what has been observed. It aims to strip away all that would stand in the way of a neutral, judgment-free presentation of the facts.

THE IDEA OF THE HOLY

Some scholars have gone beyond this simple presentation of the facts and claimed more. A classic example is Rudolf Otto's (1869–1937) book *Das Heilige* (*The Idea of the Holy*, 1917). On the basis of his study of religions, Otto claimed that central to all religious expression is an a priori sense of 'the numinous' or 'the holy'. This, of course, necessarily goes beyond a simple presentation of the facts of religious history to the development of a particular philosophical interpretation of those facts. The central truth of all religion, claimed Otto, is a genuine feeling of awe or reverence in the believer, a sense of the 'uncanny' inspired by an encounter with the divine. Otto did more than simply relate facts about religion; he assumed the existence of the holy – accepting the truth of encounters with the supernatural.

> 'Numinous dread' or awe characterizes the so-called 'religion of primitive man', where it appears as 'daemonic dread.'
>
> Rudolf Otto, *The Idea of the Holy*

For some scholars, for example Ninian Smart, such an assumption is unacceptable in the study of religion. To compromise objectivity in this way, Smart argued, skews the scholar's research and findings. What the scholar ends up with is not an unbiased account of the facts of religion, but a personal *theology* of religion.

NEUTRALITY

Whilst Otto's type of phenomenology clearly displays a basic lack of objectivity, it is now generally recognized that this is a problem intrinsic to the study of religions. Although many contemporary religious studies scholars would want to defend the notion of *epoché* as an ideal to which one should aspire, there is a question as to whether this ideal involves a certain naivety. For example, the very process of selection and production of typologies assumes a level of interpretation. To select certain facts rather than others, and to present them with other facts as a particular type of religion, presupposes some interpretation. What facts we consider important and unimportant, interesting or uninteresting, will be shaped by certain ideas that we hold, whether religious or non-religious. To be an atheist does not in itself make the scholar more objective and neutral. Hence, the belief in detached objectivity, and the claim to be purely 'descriptive', are now considered to be naive. The important thing is that, as we engage in study, we recognize and critically evaluate our beliefs, our presuppositions, our biases, and how they might shape the way we understand a religion (see 'Critical Theory and Religion').

INSIDERS AND OUTSIDERS

Another important issue in contemporary religious studies is the 'insider/outsider' problem. To what extent can a non-believer ('an outsider') understand a faith in the way the believer (an 'insider') does? It is argued that outsiders, simply because they are outsiders, will never fully grasp the insider's experience; even people who experience the same event at the same time will, because of their contexts and personal histories, interpret that experience in different ways. However, some scholars have insisted there is a definite advantage to studying religion from the outside — sometimes referred to as the 'etic' perspective. Members of a religion may be conditioned by, or pressurized into accepting, a particular — and often narrow — understanding of their faith, whereas the outsider is in the scholarly position of not being influenced by such pressures and conditioning. Impartiality and disinterest allow greater objectivity.

There is undoubtedly value in scholarly detachment. However — while the scholar may have a greater knowledge of the history, texts, philosophy, structure, and social implications of a particular faith than the average believer — not to have experienced that faith from the inside is surely to have a rather large hole in the centre of one's understanding. Indeed, many insiders will insist that scholarly 'head-knowledge' is peripheral to the 'meaning' of their faith. Hence, others have noted the value of studying a religion as an 'insider', or at least relying heavily on the views of insiders — sometimes referred to as the 'emic' perspective.

RESPONSE THRESHOLD

In order to take account of the emic perspective, along with the emphasis on participant observation (see 'The Anthropology of Religion'), some have spoken of the 'response threshold' in religious studies. The crossing of the response threshold happens when insiders question the scholar's interpretations: etic interpretations are challenged by emic perspectives. An insider's perspective – which may conflict with scholarly interpretations – is felt to carry equal, if not more, weight. Wilfred Cantwell Smith (1916–2000) has even argued that no understanding of a faith is valid until it has been acknowledged by an insider. Religious studies are thus carried out in the context of a dialogue which takes seriously the views of the insider, in order to gain a deeper understanding of the insider's world view.

BEYOND PHENOMENOLOGY

In his book entitled *Beyond Phenomenology* (1999), Gavin Flood has argued that what is important in studying religions is 'not so much the distinction between the insider and the outsider, but between the critical and the non-critical'. Flood makes use of theories developed within the social sciences and humanities. With reference to the shift in contemporary theoretical discourse, which recognizes that all knowledge is tradition-specific and embodied within particular cultures (see 'Critical Theory and Religion'), Flood argues, firstly, that religions should not be abstracted and studied apart from the historical, political, cultural, linguistic, and social contexts. Secondly, he argues that scholars, who are likewise shaped by their own contexts, always bring conceptual baggage to the study of religion. Hence, whether because of the effect research has on the community being studied, or because the scholar's own prejudices, preconceptions, instincts, emotions, and personal characteristics significantly influence that research, the academic study of religion can never be neutral and purely objective. Flood thus argues for 'a rigorous metatheoretical discourse' in religious studies. Metatheory is the critical analysis of theory and practice, the aim of which is to 'unravel the underlying assumptions inherent in any research programme and to critically comment on them'.

Metatheory is thus important because it 'questions the contexts of inquiry, the nature of inquiry, and the kinds of interests represented in inquiry'. In so doing, it questions the idea of detached objectivity in the study of religion, and the notion that one can be a disinterested observer who is able to produce neutral descriptions of religious phenomena, free of evaluative judgments. Hence, scholars need always to engage critically with, and take account of, their own assumptions, prejudices, and presuppositions.

This means that holding a particular faith need not be a hindrance to the study of religion. One can, for example, be a Christian theologian and a good student of religion. But for scholars such as Flood, the important thing is not the faith or lack of it, but the awareness of, and the critical engagement with, one's assumptions: 'It is critique rather than faith that is all important.'

It is worth noting that recent work, mainly in France, sees new possibilities for the philosophy of religion through a turn to phenomenology. Much of this work has been done in response to the important French Jewish philosopher Emmanuel Levinas (1905–95). The names particularly associated with this turn are Jean-Luc Marion, Dominique Janicaud, Jean-Luc Chretien, Michel Henry, and Alain Badiou. Marion, for example, has written on the phenomenology of the gift in theology, Badiou has responded to Levinas arguing against his emphasis on the importance of 'the other', and Chretien has written on the phenomenology of prayer.

CHRISTOPHER PARTRIDGE

CHAPTER 3

The Anthropology of Religion

Anthropology approaches religion as an aspect of culture. Religious beliefs and practices are important because they are central to the ways in which we organize our social lives. They shape our understanding of our place in the world, and determine how we relate to one another and to the rest of the natural, and supernatural, order. The truth or falsity of religious beliefs, or the authenticity or moral worth of religious practices, are seldom an issue for anthropologists, whose main concern is to document what people think and do, rather than determine what they ought to believe, or how they should behave.

RELIGION AND SOCIAL STRUCTURE

An early observation in the anthropology of religion was the extent to which religion and social structure mirror one another. Both the French historian Fustel de Coulanges (1830–89), drawing on Classical sources, and the Scottish biblical scholar William Robertson Smith (1846–94), who studied Semitic religions, demonstrated this coincidence in form. For example, nomadic peoples such as the Bedouin conceive of God in terms

> The belief in a supreme God or a single God is no mere philosophical speculation; it is a great practical idea.
>
> Maurice Hocart

of a father, and use familial and pastoral imagery to describe their relationship with God. A settled, hierarchical society, by contrast, will depict God as a monarch to whom tribute is due, with imagery of servants and subjects honouring a supreme ruler. These early studies influenced the French sociologist Émile Durkheim (1858–1917), whose book *The Elementary Forms of the Religious Life* (1912) was foundational for later anthropological studies of religion. Rather than seeing religion as determining social structure, Durkheim argued that religion is a projection of society's highest values and goals. The realm of the sacred is separated from the profane world and made to seem both natural and obligatory. Through collective rituals people both reaffirm their belief in supernatural beings and reinforce their bonds with one another.

The totemism of Australian Aboriginals, which links human groups with particular forms of animal or other natural phenomena in relations of prohibition and prescription, was regarded by many nineteenth-century scholars as the earliest form of religion, and as such was of interest to both Durkheim and the anthropologist Edward Burnett Tylor

(1832–1917), who postulated an evolutionary movement from animism to polytheism and then monotheism. However, as evolutionary arguments are essentially unprovable, later work built not on these foundations, but on the more sociological insights of Durkheim and anthropologists such as Alfred Radcliffe-Brown (1881–1955) and Sir Edward Evan Evans-Pritchard (1902–73).

Evans-Pritchard sought to retain the historical perspective of his predecessors, while replacing speculation concerning origins with data based on first-hand observations and participation in the life of a people. His classic 1937 ethnography of witchcraft, oracles, and magic among the Azande in Central Africa demonstrated that beliefs which, from a Western perspective, appear irrational and unscientific – such as the existence of witches and magic – are perfectly logical, once one understands the ideational system on which a society is based.

SYMBOLISM

While Durkheim was avowedly atheist, some of the most influential anthropologists of the later twentieth century, including Evans-Pritchard, were or became practising Roman Catholics. This is true of Mary Douglas (1921–2007) and Victor Turner (1920–83), both of whom were particularly interested in the symbolic aspects of religion. They were influenced not only by Durkheim and Evans-Pritchard, but more particularly by Durkheim's gifted pupils Marcel Mauss (1872–1950) and Henri Hubert (1864–1925), who wrote on ceremonial exchange, sacrifice, and magic.

> *Man is an animal suspended in webs of significance he himself has spun. I take culture to be those webs.*
>
> Clifford Geertz, *The Interpretation of Cultures: Selected Essays* (New York, 1973)

In her influential collection of essays *Purity and Danger* (1966), Douglas looked at the ways in which the human body is used as a symbol system in which meanings are encoded. The body is seen as a microcosm of the powers and dangers attributed to society at large. Thus, a group that is concerned to maintain its social boundaries, such as members of the Brahman caste in India, pays great attention to notions of purity and pollution as they affect the individual body. In examining purity rules, Douglas was primarily concerned with systems of classification. In her study of the Hebrew purity rules in the book of Leviticus, for example, Douglas argued that dietary proscriptions were not the result of medical or hygiene concerns, but followed the logic of a system of classification that divided animals into clean and unclean species according to whether they conformed to certain rules – such as being cloven-hooved and chewing cud – or were anomalous, and therefore unclean and prohibited. Like Robertson Smith, Douglas observed that rituals can retain their form over many generations, notwithstanding changes in their interpretation, and that meaning is preserved in the form itself, as well as in explanations for a particular ritual action.

In the work of Mary Douglas we see a fruitful combination of the sociological and symbolist tradition of the Durkheimians and the structuralism of Claude Lévi-Strauss (1908–2009). Lévi-Strauss carried out some fieldwork in the Amazonian region of Brazil, but it is as a theoretician that he has been most influential, looking not at the meaning or semantics of social structure, but at its syntax or formal aspects. In his four-volume study of mythology (1970–81), he sought to demonstrate the universality of certain cultural themes, often expressed as binary oppositions, such as the transformation of food from raw to cooked, or the opposition between culture and nature. The structuralism of Lévi-Strauss both looks back to Russian formalism and the linguistics of the Swiss Ferdinand de Saussure (1857–1913), and forwards to more recent psychoanalytic studies of religion, both of which see themselves as belonging more to a scientific than to a humanist tradition.

RITUAL AND SYMBOL

On the symbolist and interpretive side, Victor Turner (1920–83) produced a series of sensitive, detailed studies of ritual and symbols, focusing on the processual nature of ritual and its theatrical, dramatic aspects, based on extensive fieldwork among the Ndembu of Zambia carried out in the 1950s. Clifford Geertz (1926–2006) was equally concerned with meaning and interpretation, and following a German-American tradition he looked more at culture than at social structure. Geertz saw religion as essentially that which gives meaning to human society, and religious symbols as codifying an ethos or world view. Their power lies in their ability both to reflect and to shape society.

Recently, important changes have stemmed from postmodernism and postcolonial thinking, globalization and multiculturalism. Anthropologists now often incorporate a critique of their own position and interests into their studies, and are no longer preoccupied exclusively with 'exotic' small-scale societies; for instance, there is a lot of research into global Pentecostalism and its local forms. The impact of new forms of media in the religious sphere has also become a significant area of study.

FIONA BOWIE

MYTHS AND SYMBOLS

One dimension of religions which has received particular attention by scholars has been that of myths and symbols. If we had just heard a moving piece of music, we would find it strange if someone asked us whether the music were true or false. Music, we might reply, is neither true nor false; to ask such a question is inappropriate. Most people know that music can, as it were, speak to them, even though no words are used.

As with music so with people. The question of what someone 'means' to you cannot fully be answered by saying that he is your husband or she is your wife, because there are always unspoken levels of intuition, feeling, and emotion built into relationships. The question of 'meaning' must always be seen to concern these dimensions, as well as the more obviously factual ones.

Myths

Myths take many forms, depending on the culture in which they are found. But their function is always that of pinpointing vital issues and values in the life of the society concerned. They often dramatize those profound issues of life and death, of how humanity came into being, and of what life means, of how we should conduct ourselves as a citizen or spouse, as a creature of God or as a farmer, and so on.

Myths are not scientific or sociological theories about these issues; they are the outcome of the way a nation or group has pondered the great questions. Their function is not merely to provide a theory of life that can be taken or left at will; they serve to compel a response from humanity. We might speak of myths as bridges between the intellect and emotion, between the mind and heart – and in this, myths are like music. They express an idea and trigger our response to it.

Sometimes myths form an extensive series, interlinking with each other and encompassing many aspects of life, as has been shown for the Dogon people of the River Niger in West Africa. On the other hand, they may serve merely as partial accounts of problems, such as the hatred between people and snakes, or the reason for the particular shape of a mountain.

One problem in our understanding of myths lies in the fact that the so-called Western religions – Judaism, Christianity, and Islam – are strongly concerned with history. They have founders, and see their history as God's own doing. This strong emphasis upon actual events differs from the Eastern approaches to religion, which emphasize the consciousness of the individual. Believing in the cyclical nature of time, Hinduism and Buddhism possess a different approach to history, and hence also to science.

In the West, the search for facts in science is like the search for facts in history, but both these endeavours differ from the search for religious experience in the present. In the West, history and science have come to function as a framework within which religious experiences are found and interpreted, one consequence of which is that myths are often no longer appreciated for their power to evoke human responses to religious ideas.

The eminent historian of religion Mircea Eliade (1907–86) sought to restore this missing sense of the sacred by helping people to understand the true nature of myths. The secularized Westerner has lost the sense of the sacred, and is trying to compensate, as Eliade saw it, by means of science fiction, supernatural literature, and films. One may, of course, keep a firm sense of history and science without seeking to destroy the mythical appreciation of ideas and beliefs.

Symbols

Religious symbols help believers to understand their faith in quite profound ways. Like myths, they serve to unite the intellect and the emotions. Symbols also integrate the social and personal dimensions of religion, enabling individuals to share certain commonly held beliefs expressed by symbols, while also giving freedom to read private meaning into them.

We live the whole of our life in a world of symbols. The daily smiles and grimaces, handshakes and greetings, as well as the more readily acknowledged status symbols of large cars or houses – all these communicate messages about ourselves to others.

To clarify the meaning of symbols, it will help if we distinguish between the terms 'symbol' and 'sign'. There is a certain arbitrariness about signs, so that the word 'table', which signifies an object of furniture with a flat top supported on legs, could be swapped for another sound without any difficulty. Thus the Germans call it *tisch* and the Welsh *bwrdd*.

A symbol, by contrast, is more intimately involved in that to which it refers. It participates in what it symbolizes, and cannot easily be swapped for another symbol. Nor can it be explained in words and still carry the same power. For example, a kiss is a symbol of affection and love; it not only signifies these feelings in some abstract way; it actually demonstrates them. In this sense a symbol can be a thought in action.

Religious symbols share these general characteristics, but are often even more intensely powerful, because they enshrine and express the highest values and relationships of life. The cross of Christ, the sacred books of Muslims and Sikhs, the sacred cow of Hindus, or the silent, seated Buddha – all these command the allegiance of millions of religious men and women. If such symbols are attacked or desecrated, an intense reaction is felt by the faithful, which shows us how deeply symbols are embedded in the emotional life of believers.

The power of symbols lies in this ability to unite fellow-believers into a community. It provides a focal point of faith and action, while also making possible a degree of personal understanding which those outside may not share.

In many societies the shared aspect of symbols is important as a unifying principle of life. Blood, for example, may be symbolic of life, strength, parenthood, or of the family and kinship group itself. In Christianity it expresses life poured out in death, the self-sacrificial love of Christ who died for human sin. It may even be true that the colour red can so easily serve as a symbol of

The cross is the central symbol of Christianity.

danger because of its deeper biological association with life and death.

Symbols serve as triggers of commitment in religions. They enshrine the teachings and express them in a tangible way. So the sacraments of baptism and the Lord's Supper in Christianity bring the believer into a practical relationship with otherwise abstract ideas, such as repentance and forgiveness. People can hardly live without symbols because they always need something to motivate life; it is as though abstract ideas need to be set within a symbol before individuals can be impelled to act upon them. When any attempt is made to turn symbols into bare statements of truth, this vital trigger of the emotions can easily be lost.

Douglas Davies

CHAPTER 4

The Sociology of Religion

The sociological study of religion has its roots in the seventeenth- and eighteenth-century Enlightenment, when a number of influential thinkers sought not only to question religious belief, but also to understand it as a natural phenomenon, a human product rather than the result of divine revelation or revealed truth. While contemporary sociology of religion has largely abandoned the overtly critical stance of early theoretical approaches to the truth claims of religion, the discipline retains the essential principle that an understanding of religion must acknowledge that it is, to some degree at least, socially constructed, and that social processes are fundamentally involved in the emergence, development, and dissemination of religious beliefs and practices.

METHODOLOGICAL AGNOSTICISM

While some sociologists consider that some religious beliefs are false, and that recognition of this is crucial to a sociological understanding of them, the dominant position in the sociology of religion today is that of 'methodological agnosticism'. This method states that it is neither possible, nor necessary, to decide whether beliefs are true or false in order to study them sociologically. Theology and philosophy of religion, not sociology, discuss questions of religious truth. The conditions which promote the acceptance or rejection of religious beliefs and practices, which govern their dissemination and the impact they have on behaviour and on society, can all be investigated without prior determination of their truth or falsity.

ROOTS IN INDIVIDUAL NEEDS

Theoretical approaches in the sociology of religion can usefully – if a little crudely – be divided into those which perceive the roots of religion to lie in individual needs and propensities, and those which perceive its roots to lie in social processes and to stem from the characteristics of society and social groups. The former may be further divided into those which emphasize cognitive processes – intellectualism – and those which emphasize various feelings and emotions – emotionalism.

In the nineteenth century, intellectualist theorists such as Auguste Comte (1798–1857), Edward Burnett Tylor (1832–1917), James G. Frazer (1854–1941), and Herbert Spencer (1820–1903) analyzed religious belief as essentially a pre-scientific attempt to understand the world and human experience, which would increasingly be supplanted by sound scientific knowledge. The future would thus be entirely secular, with no place for religion.

Emotionalist theorists, such as Robert Ranulph Marett (1866–1943), Bronislaw Malinowski (1884–1942), and Sigmund Freud (1856–1939), saw religions as stemming from human emotions such as fear, uncertainty, ambivalence, and awe. They were not attempts to explain and understand, but to cope with intense emotional experience.

ROOTS IN SOCIAL PROCESSES

The most influential sociological approaches that consider the roots of religion lie in society and social processes, not in the individual, are those of Karl Marx (1818–83) and Émile Durkheim (1858–1917).

For Marx, religion was both a form of ideology supported by ruling classes in order to control the masses, and at the same time an expression of protest against such oppression – 'the sigh of the oppressed creature'. As a protest, however, it changed nothing, promoting only resignation, and promising resolution of problems in the afterlife. Religion is 'the opium of the people', in the sense that it dulls the pain of the oppressed and thereby stops them from revolting. Hence, the oppressed turn to religion to help them get through life; the ruling classes promote it to keep them in check. It will simply disappear when the social conditions that cause it are removed.

> *Religion is the sigh of the oppressed creature and the opium of the people.*
>
> Karl Marx, *A Contribution to the Critique of Hegel's Philosophy of Right* (Deutsch-Französische Jahrbücher, 1844).

Durkheim saw religion as an essential, integrating social force, which fulfilled basic functions in society. It was the expression of human subordination, not to a ruling class, as Marx had argued, but rather to the requirements of society itself, and to social pressures which overrule individual preferences. In his famous work *The Elementary Forms of the Religious Life* (1912), Durkheim argued that 'Religion is society worshipping itself'. God may not exist, but society does; rather than God exerting pressure on the individual to conform, society itself exerts the pressure. Individuals, who do not understand the nature of society and social groups, use the language of religion to explain the social forces they experience. Although people misinterpret social forces as religious forces, what they experience is real. Moreover, for Durkheim, religion fulfils a positive role, in that it binds society together as a moral community.

MAX WEBER AND MEANING THEORY

Later theoretical approaches in the sociology of religion have all drawn extensively on this earlier work, attempting to synthesize its insights into more nuanced approaches, in which the various strands of intellectual, emotional, and social factors are woven together. A notable example is the work of Max Weber (1864–1920), probably the most significant contributor to the sociology of religion to this day. His work included one of the best-known treatises in the sub-discipline, *The Protestant Ethic and the Spirit of Capitalism* (1904–05), and three major studies of world religions.

Weber's approach to religion was the forerunner of what has become known as 'meaning theory', which emphasizes the way in which religion gives meaning to human life and society, in the face of apparently arbitrary suffering and injustice. Religion offers explanation and justification of good and of bad fortune, by locating them within a broader picture of a reality which may go beyond the world of immediate everyday perception, thereby helping to make sense of what always threatens to appear senseless. So those who suffer undeservedly in this life may have offended in a previous one; or they will receive their just deserts in the next life, or in heaven. Those who prosper through wickedness will ultimately be judged and duly punished.

RATIONAL CHOICE THEORY

The most recent, general theoretical approach in the sociology of religion, which synthesizes many previous insights, is that of 'rational choice theory'. Drawing upon economic theory, this treats religions as rival products offered in a market by religious organizations – which are compared to commercial firms – and leaders, to consumers, who choose by assessing which best meets their needs, which is most reliable, and so on. This approach promises to provide many insights. However, it has been subjected to trenchant criticism by those who question whether religion can be treated as something chosen in the way that products such as cars or soap-powders are chosen, rather than something into which people are socialized, and which forms an important part of their identity that cannot easily be set aside or changed. Furthermore, if religious beliefs are a matter of preference and convenience, why do their followers accept the uncongenial demands and constraints they usually impose, and the threat of punishments for failure to comply?

SECULARIZATION AND NEW MOVEMENTS

The sociology of religion was for many decades regarded as an insignificant branch of sociology. This situation has changed in recent years, especially in the USA. Substantive empirical inquiry has been dominated by two areas: secularization and religious sects, cults, and movements. It had been widely assumed that religion was declining in modern industrial societies and losing its social significance – the secularization thesis. This has

Hare Krishna Festival of Chariots in Trafalgar Square, London. Hare Krishna is one of many New Religious Movements.

been questioned and found by many — especially rational choice theorists — to be wanting. The result has been intense debate. The dominant position now, though not unchallenged, is that the secularization thesis was a myth.

Central to this debate is the claim that — while religion in its traditional forms may be declining in some modern, Western industrial societies — it is not declining in all of them, the USA being a notable exception; and that novel forms of religion are continuously emerging to meet inherent spiritual needs. Some new forms are clearly religious in character. Others, it is claimed, are quite unlike religion as commonly understood, and include alternative and complementary forms of healing, psychotherapies, techniques for the development of human potential, deep ecology, holistic spirituality, New Age, the cult of celebrity, nationalist movements, and even sport. Whether such things can be considered forms of religion depends upon how religion is defined, a matter much disputed.

A second crucial element in the secularization debate is the rise of a diversity of sects and cults – the New Religious Movements – which have proliferated since the 1960s and 1970s. For the anti-secularization – or 'sacralization' – theorists, this flourishing of novel religiosity gives the lie to the thesis; while for pro-secularization theorists, such movements fall far short of making up for the decline of mainstream churches and denominations. Whatever their significance for the secularization thesis, the New Religious Movements – and sects and cults in general – have fascinated sociologists, whose extensive studies of them form a major part of the subject.

Heavy concentration on New Religious Movements has been balanced more recently by studies of more mainstream religious churches and communities, and by studies of the religious life of ethnic minorities and immigrant communities, among whom religion is often particularly significant and an important element of identity. Added to the interest in new forms of religion and quasi-religion, such studies make the contemporary sociology of religion more diverse and varied than ever.

MALCOLM HAMILTON

CHAPTER 5

The Psychology of Religion

Three key figures dominate the psychology of religion that we have inherited from the pre-World War II period: William James, Sigmund Freud, and C. G. Jung.

WILLIAM JAMES (1842–1910)

The undoubted masterpiece of the early days of the psychology of religion is the classic *Varieties of Religious Experience*, written by William James at the end of the nineteenth century. James assembled an interesting compendium of personal reports of religious experience, and embedded them in a rich and subtle framework of analysis. He thought religious experience was essentially an individual matter, the foundation on which religious doctrine and church life were built. However, from the outset his critics argued that religious experience is in fact interpreted within the framework of inherited religious teaching and shaped by the life of the institution. James hoped to put religion on a scientific basis, through the scientific study of religious experience, although he was unable to make a really convincing case for accepting religious experience at face value. Despite these issues, even his critics have never doubted the quality of his work, which is as hotly debated now as when it was first written.

SIGMUND FREUD (1856–1939)

Another important figure in the development of the psychology of religion was Sigmund Freud, although his approach was very different from that of James. Freud built his general theories upon what patients told him during their psychoanalysis, although he reported only one case study in which religion played a central part. This was the so-called 'wolf man', in whom religion and obsessionality were intertwined, which led Freud to suggest that religion was a universal form of obsessional neurosis. In fact, Freud's psychology of religion was hardly based on data at all; it was a blend of general psychoanalytic theory and his own personal hostility to religion. He wrote several books about religion, each taking a different approach. The clearest is *The Future of an Illusion*, which claims that religion is merely 'illusion', which for him is a technical term meaning wish-fulfilment.

Freud's successors have argued that what he called illusion, including religion, is in fact much more valuable than he realized to people in helping them to adjust to life.

C. G. JUNG (1875–1961)

Freud's approach to religion was continued in modified form by Carl Gustav Jung. Whereas Freud had been a harsh critic of religion, Jung was favourably disposed to it. However, his approach to religion was so idiosyncratic that many have found him an uncomfortable friend. Jung made a distinction between the ego – the centre of conscious life – and the self – the whole personality that people can potentially become. For Jung, the self is the image of God in the psyche, and the process of 'individuation' – that is, development from

Sigmund Freud (1856–1939).

ego-centred life to self-centred life – is in some ways analogous to religious salvation. Jung was evasive about the question of whether there was a god beyond the psyche, and usually said it was not a question for him as a psychologist. Jung took more interest in the significance of Christian doctrine than most psychologists and, for example, wrote long essays on the Mass and on the Trinity.

> *Religious ideas … are illusions, fulfilments of the oldest, strongest, and most urgent wishes of mankind.*
>
> Sigmund Freud, *The Future of an Illusion* (London: Hogarth, 1962).

THE PSYCHOLOGY OF RELIGION TODAY

The psychology of religion went relatively quiet around the middle of the twentieth century, but has been reviving in recent decades. It has become more explicitly scientific, and most psychological research on religion now uses quantitative methods. There are currently no big psychological theories of religion, but important insights have been obtained about various specific aspects of religion. The following examples give a flavour of current work.

- *Individual differences.* One useful distinction has been between 'intrinsic' religious people – those for whom religion is the dominant motivation in their lives – and 'extrinsic' religious people – those for whom religion meets other needs. Intrinsics and extrinsics differ from one another in many ways. For example, it has been suggested that intrinsically religious people show less social prejudice than non-religious people, whereas extrinsically religious people show more.

- *Religious development.* Children's understanding of religion follows a predictable path, moving from the concrete to the abstract. However, acquiring a better intellectual understanding of religion is not necessarily accompanied by a more spiritual experience. In fact, spiritual experience may actually decline as children grow up. There have been attempts to extend a development approach to religion into adulthood. For example, James Fowler developed a general theory of 'faith development'. Although this has identified different approaches to faith in adults, it is not clear that higher levels of faith necessarily follow the earlier ones, nor that they are superior.
- *Mental health.* Despite Freud's view that religion is a form of neurosis, scientific research has shown that there is often a positive correlation between religion and health, especially mental health. It is most likely that religion actually helps to improve people's mental health, although this is hard to prove conclusively. Religion probably helps by providing a framework of meaning and a supportive community, both of which enable people to cope better with stressful experiences.
- *Conservative and charismatic Christianity.* There has been much interest in both fundamentalism and charismatic religion. One key feature of fundamentalism is the 'black and white' mindset that maintains a sharp dichotomy between truth and falsehood, and between insiders and outsiders. The charismatic phenomenon that has attracted most research interest is speaking in tongues. It seems very unlikely that this is an actual language; it is probably more a form of ecstatic utterance. One line of research has explored the social context in which people learn to speak in tongues, and another the unusual state of consciousness in which people surrender voluntary control of their speech.

Although psychology has generally taken a detached, scientific view of religion, there are other points of contact. One is the incorporation of psychological methods into the Christian church's pastoral care, begun by Freud's Lutheran pastor friend, Oskar Pfister (1873–1956). Another is the dialogue between religious and psychological world-views, an aspect of the more general dialogue between science and religion. Some psychologists consider that humans are 'nothing but' the product of their evolution or their nervous systems, whereas religious faith emphasizes their importance in the purposes of God.

FRASER WATTS

CHAPTER 6

Theological Approaches to the Study of Religion

During the development of the study of religion as a new discipline in the twentieth century, the pioneers of the field were often at pains to stress that what they did was different from theology. As such, it might be asked whether a theological approach even belongs within the study of religion. Many scholars today, who emphasize it as a scientific or historical discipline, distance themselves from any notion that theology, in any form, has a place within the study of religion. For others, the relationship is more ambiguous, while some scholars even argue that theological approaches are essential to understanding, and so truly studying, religion.

WHAT DO WE MEAN BY 'THEOLOGY'?

It is best to start by defining what we mean by 'theology' in relation to the study of religion. We will begin with some negatives. First, it does not mean a confessional approach, where the teachings of one school, tradition, or sect within a religion are taught as the true, or correct, understanding of that religion. Second, theology does not imply that there is any need for a belief, or faith content, within the person studying in that idiom. It is not, therefore, under the classic definition of the medieval Christian Anselm of Canterbury (1033–1109), an act of 'faith seeking understanding'.

We come now to the positives. First, it is about understanding the internal terms within which a religion will seek to explain itself, its teachings, and its formulations. We must be clear here that 'theology' is used loosely, because while it makes sense as a Christian term – literally it is the study of God – and can be fairly clearly applied to other theistic traditions, it is also used elsewhere to talk about broadly philosophical traditions related to transcendence. Accordingly, people use the term 'Buddhist theology' – although others question whether this usage is appropriate, but space does not permit us to engage in such disputes here. Second, it means engaging with empathy with questions of meaning as they would make sense within the religious worldview, and so goes beyond reasoning and relates to a way of life. Here, we see clear resonances with phenomenological approaches, where we seek to understand a religion on its own terms.

Anselm of Canterbury (1033–1109).

Indeed, without a theological viewpoint, it can be argued that the study of religions fails, because on the one hand it is either simply reductionist, that is to say it explains via some chosen system why the religion exists, what it does, and what it means — as tends to be the case with some parts of the sociology or psychology of religion. Or, on the other hand, it becomes merely descriptive, telling us what rituals are performed, what the ethics are, what the teachings are, how it is lived out, and so on — a simply phenomenological approach. A theological approach looks into the religion, and seeks to understand what it means to believers within its own terms, and how that system works as a rational worldview to those within it.

INSIDER AND OUTSIDER

Two important pairs of distinctions are useful to consider how theological approaches are applied. The first, developed by the anthropologist Kenneth Pike (1912–2000), and often applied to religion, concerns what are called 'emic' and 'etic' approaches. An emic approach attempts to explain things within the cultural world of the believer. An etic approach is the way an external observer would try and make sense of the behaviours and beliefs of a society or group in some form of scientific sense. Within anthropology, these basic distinctions are seen as part of the tools of the trade. Unless she enters into the thought-world of a group, culture, and society, the anthropologist will remain forever exterior, and will not understand what things mean to those in that group. Moreover, emic understandings can help inspire etic description, and assess its appropriateness. Clearly, in the study of religion, this originally anthropological distinction suggests that an emic, or theological, approach is justified.

Our second pair of distinctions is the notion of 'Insider' and 'Outsider' perspectives. These are, respectively, concepts from somebody who is a believer (an Insider), and a non-believer, that is, the scholar (an Outsider). This differs from the emic/etic distinction, because they are always perspectives of the Outsider: the scholar. As such, an emic theological approach is different from the confessional theology of an Insider. However, this distinction is often blurred. Field anthropologists speak of spending so much time within the group or society they study that they often almost become part of that group, and part of good fieldwork is about entering the life world of those studied. This applies equally to scholars of religion, especially those engaged in fieldwork.

Another issue is that scholars may be believers within a religion, and so may inhabit both Insider and Outsider worlds. This raises many interesting questions, but here we will note simply that the notion of the detached, impartial, and objective scholar is increasingly questioned. Issues raised by critical theory have suggested that every standpoint will always have a bias, and some have argued further – notably the Hindu scholar, Gavin Flood – that a religious point of view, if openly acknowledged, can form part of the broader study of religions. Moreover, religious groups are often affected by what scholars of religion say about them. Therefore, Insider worldviews and Outsider descriptions – etic or emic – become intertwined in a dance that affects each other. As such, the question of how a theological approach fits into, or works within, religious studies is far from simple.

ALWAYS 'TAINTED'?

Scholars such as Timothy Fitzgerald, Tomoko Masuzawa, and Tala Asad have argued that the supposedly secular study of religion has always been 'tainted', because it developed in a world where Christianity dominated – often with a particular kind of liberal theology – so that no study of religion is entirely free from theology. Certainly, some foundational figures, such as Mircea Eliade, had a religious worldview, and a lot of mid-twentieth century work developing the phenomenology of religion, or comparative religion, made assumptions about a religious realm that underlay all traditions. However, it is arguable whether all scholars of religion then and since are affected in this way, while a case can be made that it was not solely Christian assumptions that affected the study of religion, but that such assumptions were shaped by the encounter with various religious traditions. As such, while we must be suspicious of some categories within the study of religion, we do not need to assume that everything has a Christian basis. Indeed, Frank Whaling argues we must also not forget that many religions have a lot to say about other religions, and this leads into theorizing on comparative religion, comparative theology, and the theology of religions within a confessional standpoint which is not entirely separate from understanding a religion and its worldview.

The relationship of the study of religions and theology varies in different countries. For instance, in Germany the two tend to be starkly polarized, with theology departments being — at least traditionally — strictly confessional, normally Roman Catholic or Protestant, and the study of religions — understood as a primarily reductionist secular discipline — is always separate from theology. In the UK, the ancient universities started to admit non-Anglican Christian denominations from the nineteenth century, and so lost their confessional stance, with seminaries for training priests becoming separate or linked institutions. For this reason, it was easier to start teaching theology from a generic standpoint, which could integrate other religions as part of the curriculum, and so there are many combined departments for theology and the study of religion. The USA tends to have a more separate system, although there are places where an active study of religion discipline exists within a theology department. Obviously, such regional differences affect the way a theological approach to the study of religion is accepted or understood.

PAUL HEDGES

CHAPTER 7

Critical Theory and Religion

Our knowledge of 'religion' is always politically shaped, and never an innocent or a neutral activity. Knowledge about religion can always be questioned, and scholars of religion are finding that 'religion', and talk about 'religion', is involved with questions of power. Critical theory questions knowledge about 'religion', and reveals the social and political nature of such ideas.

DEFINING CRITICAL THEORY

Critical theory arises from a long tradition in Western thought which has questioned the truth and certainty of knowledge. It carries forward the work of the 'three great masters of suspicion', Karl Marx (1818–83), Friedrich Nietzsche (1844–1900), and Sigmund Freud (1856–1939). Following Marx, critical theory is aware that all knowledge is linked to economic and political ideology; following Nietzsche, it understands that all knowledge is linked to the 'will to power'; and following Freud, it understands that all knowledge is linked to things outside our awareness (the unconscious). The ideas of these three great thinkers influence, and are carried forward in, the work of critical theory. All three started to question the view that knowledge was neutral and rational.

Friedrich Nietzsche (1844–1900).

There are two basic understandings of 'critical theory', a strict definition and a loose definition. The former relates to the Frankfurt School of Critical Theory, an important group of German intellectuals who tried to think about society according to the ideas of Marx and Freud.

They included Theodor Adorno (1903–69) and Max Horkheimer (1895–1973), who jointly published *Dialectic of Enlightenment*, a seminal work in which they questioned Western rational thought since the Enlightenment. What did it say about the potential of human knowledge if it could lead to the ideology of Nazi Germany and the horrors of the Holocaust? Culture was understood to be formed by propagandist manipulation.

The loose definition incorporates a wider range of critical theories, which emerged – largely in France – after the student riots of 1968 in Paris. This date is a watershed in modern Western intellectual history because it reflects, among many things, a shift in the thinking about state power and the control of ideas. It was an event that brought the questions of 'power' and 'politics' to the question of knowledge and truth.

POST-STRUCTURALISM

The critical thinking that emerged in 1968 in France is known as 'post-structuralism' because it comes after an intellectual movement known as 'structuralism'. Structuralism held that one could identify a given number of structures in myth, language, and the world. Post-structuralists argued that these structures were not 'given' in the fabric of the world, but created by different societies at different points of history and in different cultures. Michel Foucault (1926–84) examined the historical nature of ideas, showing that the ways we think about the world are related to political institutions and regimes of power. Jacques Derrida (1930–2004) showed that our ways of representing the world in texts holds hidden contradictions and tensions, because language is unstable and built upon assertions of power, not truth. The instability of language refers to the discovery that the meaning of words in a dictionary simply means other words, rather than something indisputable and fixed in the world, and that meanings are simply asserted or agreed, rather than having a strong foundation given for all time. These two prominent thinkers brought knowledge under question, and enabled scholars of religion to uncover how what is and what is not classified as 'religion' can benefit certain groups of people within society. Critical theory is thus not an abstract and disengaged way of thinking, but an active ethical responsibility for the world and the way we think about the world. It shows the link between ideas and political practices.

> *Religion is a political force.*
>
> Michel Foucault

THE END OF PHENOMENOLOGY

Before critical theory, the study of religion often consisted of representing different religious traditions, and understanding them according to their rituals, beliefs, and practices. This is known as 'the phenomenology of religion', and is arguably still dominant in school and university programmes of study. Such an approach assumed that knowledge is neutral, and that different issues can be presented without too much difficulty. It was also assumed by many scholars that one does not need a 'theory' or 'theoretical position' –

a way of understanding knowledge and the world – to represent a religious tradition or a set of ideas. There was an assumption that language neutrally represented the external world according to a direct correspondence between the subject in representation (words) and the object in the external world (things) – in this case 'religious' things. However, knowledge and the categories used to represent the world and religion are now seen to be carrying hidden assumptions, with implications for gender, society, politics, colonial history, race, and ethnicity. All knowledge is now seen as reflecting a particular viewpoint or bias about the world; the production and acquisition of knowledge is never neutral. Hence, after critical theory, there is no neutral presentation of ideas about religion.

Critical theory is a way of thinking about how our dominant conceptions of religion come to be dominant or hegemonic. It seeks to identify the hidden positions within our knowledge, and to recognize that all ideas about religion hold a theoretical position about knowledge, even if that position is denied or not apparent. Critical theory offers a way of exploring 'religion' through a set of critical questions about the world and the ideas under discussion. It is not limited to the study of religion, but applies to all ways of thinking about the world, and even questions the boundary between different disciplines of knowledge. Critical theory is not a sub-discipline of religious studies – like the sociology, anthropology, or psychology of religion – but cuts across all these areas and questions all types of knowledge.

Critical theory questions the very idea of 'religion' as a Western – even Christian – category that assumes that belief is more important than how people live, which in turn is used to make assumptions about what people outside Christianity believe. This is seen as a distortion of other cultures. To correct such a view, critical theory considers traditions and cultures outside the bias of such an idea, which assumes there is something special and distinctive we can call 'religion' or 'religious'. For example, scholars question the Christian missionary interpretation of other cultures, and ask whether Hinduism is a 'religion' or the culture of South Asia. In turn, we may question whether Western capitalism is a culture or a religion. Critical theory draws attention to how knowledge is related to political ideas, and questions the domination of Western ideas (particularly European-American ideas) over other ways of seeing the world in different cultures and periods of history. It explores the way ideas powerfully rule the world and the 'truth' people have about the world.

RELIGION, POWER, AND CULTURE

Critical theory shows that the ways we think about religion are bound up in questions of power. Religious studies is now involved in exploring how the history and abuses of colonialism influenced the emergence of religion as an idea; how state power, political regimes, and the globalized world of capitalism affect this process; and how the mass media alter what we mean by religion, and uncover those activities and groups within society not recognized as religious. Critical theory exposes the abuses of power in history, and examines who benefits from thinking about the world in certain ways. It identifies those who are marginalized and unable to speak for themselves.

By examining race, gender, sexuality, and economic wealth one can see how ideas about religion often support those in power, usually the ruling educated elite of white, Western men. Thinking and writing about ideas from the position of the exploited radically changes the subject and the writing of history. Such a process questions, for example, the narrative of Christian history from its Roman-European bias, and examines Christianity through its African — particularly Ethiopian — traditions, highlighting the importance of Augustine as an African. It explores the involvement of Buddhist monks in political activism, and uncovers how the Western media distort the understanding of Islam. Critical theory also identifies ways of life outside the mainstream traditions, and explores the indigenous or local traditions around the world, which are suppressed by multinational business interests for land and oil.

Critical theory questions the boundary between religion and culture, and argues that what people do — rather than what they believe — is more important in understanding. The distinction between

Orthodox priests at a Christian festival at Timket, Ethiopia.

the religious and the secular is seen as an ideological or political tool. According to this view, the category of 'religion' can be applied to all cultural activities, such as football, shopping, fashion, club-culture, and film. The historical roots of social institutions — such as government, schools, hospitals, and law — are shown to carry ideas that can be classified as religious, even if they are not transparent. Critical theory radically alters the understanding of religion and shows the importance of the idea to world history. After critical theory, the study of religion becomes a political activity, an account of how powerful organizations in different parts of the world shape the way we understand and classify the world.

JEREMY CARRETTE

CHAPTER 8

Ritual and Performance

Like myths and symbols, ritual and performance is an area that has particularly interested religious studies scholars. Ritual is patterned, formal, symbolic action. Religious ritual is usually seen as having reference to divine or transcendent beings, or perhaps ancestors, whom the participants invoke, propitiate, feed – through offering or sacrifice – worship, or otherwise communicate with. Rituals attempt to enact and deal with the central dilemmas of human existence: continuity and stability, growth and fertility, morality and immortality or transcendence. They have the potential to transform people and situations, creating a fierce warrior or docile wife, a loving servant or imperious tyrant. The ambiguity of ritual symbols, and the invocation of supernatural power, magnifies and disguises human needs and emotions. Because rituals are sometimes performed in terrifying circumstances – as in certain initiation rituals – the messages they carry act at a psycho-biological level that includes, but also exceeds, the rational mind. Symbols and sacred objects are manipulated within ritual to enhance performance and communicate ideological messages concerning the nature of the individual, society, and cosmos. Rituals are fundamental to human culture, and can be used to control, subvert, stabilize, enhance, or terrorize individuals and groups. Studying them gives us a key to an understanding and interpretation of culture.

Anthropologists and religious studies scholars sometimes look at rituals in terms of what they do. For instance, Catherine Bell (b. 1953) distinguishes between:
- rites of passage or 'life crisis' rituals
- calendrical rituals and commemorative rites
- rites of exchange or communication
- rites of affliction
- rites of feasting, fasting, festivals
- political rituals

Another approach is to focus on their explanatory value. Mircea Eliade (1907–86) was interested in ritual as a re-enactment of a primal, cosmogonic myth, bringing the past continually into the present. Robin Horton emphasizes the reality of the religious beliefs behind ritual actions. Using the Kalabari of Nigeria as an example, he insists that religious rituals have the power to move and transform participants because they express beliefs that have meaning and coherence for their adherents. Taking a lead from Durkheim (1858–1917), other scholars claim that rituals are effective because they make statements about social phenomena. Maurice Bloch, writing about circumcision rituals in Madagascar, makes the interesting observation that because a ritual is not fully a statement and not fully an action it allows its message to be simultaneously communicated and disguised. In some cases ritual symbols may be full of resonance, as Victor Turner demonstrated for Ndembu heali ng, chiefly installation, and initiation rituals in Central Africa. In other cases the performance of the ritual itself may be what matters, the content or symbolism having become redundant or forgotten over time, as Fritz Staal has argued for Vedic rituals in India.

> *No experience is too lowly to be taken up in ritual and given a lofty meaning.*
>
> Mary Douglas

PATTERNS IN RITUAL

A key figure in the study of ritual is Arnold van Gennep (1873–1957), who discerned an underlying patterning beneath a wide range of rituals. Whether we look at seasonal festivals such as Christmas, midsummer, or harvest, or 'life crisis' rituals that mark a change in status from one stage of life to another, such as birth, puberty, marriage, or mortuary rituals, we see beneath them all the threefold pattern of separation, transition, and reintegration. Van Gennep also noted that there is generally a physical passage in ritual as well as a social movement, and that the first time a ritual is celebrated it is usually more elaborate than on subsequent occasions, as it bears the weight of change of status.

Victor Turner took up van Gennep's schema, emphasizing the movement from social structure to an anti-structural position in the middle, liminal, stage of a rite of passage. In the middle stage, initiands often share certain characteristics. There is a levelling process — they may be stripped, or dressed in such a way as to erase individuality, hair may be shaved or allowed to grow long. Neophytes are often isolated from the everyday world, and may undergo certain ordeals that bind them to one another and to those initiating them. Turner coined the term 'communitas' to describe a spontaneous, immediate, and concrete relatedness that is typical of people in the liminal stage of a rite of passage. Liminality can also be institutionalized and extended almost indefinitely, as for instance in the military, monastic communities, hospitals, or asylums.

MALE AND FEMALE INITIATION

Bruce Lincoln has criticized both van Gennep and Turner's models as more relevant to male than female initiations, pointing out that women have little status in the social hierarchy, and therefore the middle stage of a woman's initiation is less likely to stress anti-structural elements. Rather than being brought low as a prelude to being elevated, her lowlier place within society is reinforced. A woman is more likely than her male counterparts to be initiated singly, and to be enclosed within a domestic space. Women are generally adorned rather than stripped, and the nature of the knowledge

passed on during initiation is likely to be mundane rather than esoteric. Rather than separation, liminality, and reintegration, Lincoln proposes that for women initiation is more likely to involve enclosure, metamorphosis or magnification, and emergence.

Malagasy children, Madagascar.

A ritual is a type of performance, but not all performances are rituals. Richard Schechner (b. 1934) has pointed out that whether a performance is to be classified as ritual or theatre depends on the context. If the purpose of a performance is to be efficacious, it is a ritual. If its purpose is to entertain, it is theatre. These are not absolute distinctions, and most performances contain elements of both efficacious intention and entertainment. At the ritual end of the continuum we are likely to have an active 'audience', who share the aims and intentions of the main actors. Time and space are sacred, and symbolically marked, and it is the end result of the action that matters — to heal, initiate, aid the deceased, or whatever it may be. In a theatrical performance, the audience is more likely to observe than participate, and the event is an end in itself. It is performed for those watching, and not for, or in the presence of, a higher power or absent other.

FIONA BOWIE

A BRIEF INTRODUCTION TO JUDAISM

QUESTIONS

1. What is a religion, and why can the term be problematic?

2. Why did many phenomenologists reject theological approaches to religion?

3. An atheist will always be a more objective student of religion than a believer. How far do you agree or disagree with this statement?

4. What problems might you encounter in studying a religion as an outsider?

5. What did Marx mean when he referred to religion as 'the sigh of the oppressed creature'?

6. How do Marx and Weber differ in their perceptions of religion?

7. Explain Durkheim's view of the role of religion in society.

8. Why has there been renewed interest in the sociology of religion in recent years?

9. What can psychology tell us about why people may hold religious beliefs?

10. How has Critical Theory influenced our understanding of religion since the 1960s?

FURTHER READING

Connolly, Peter (ed.), *Approaches to the Study of Religion*. London: Continuum, 2001.

Eliade, Mircea, *The Sacred and the Profane: The Nature of Religion*. New York: Harcourt, Brace, 1959.

Fitzgerald, Timothy, *The Ideology of Religious Studies*. Oxford: Oxford University Press, 2000.

Flood, Gavin, *Beyond Phenomenology: Rethinking the Study of Religion*. London: Cassell, 1999.

Geertz, Clifford, 'Religion as a Cultural System', in Michael Banton, ed., *Anthropological Approaches to the Study of Religion*, pp. 1–46. London: Tavistock, 1966.

Kunin, Seth D., *Religion: The Modern Theories*. Baltimore: Johns Hopkins University Press, 2003.

Levi-Strauss, Claude, *Myth and Meaning*. Toronto: University of Toronto Press, 1978.

McCutcheon, Russell T. ed., *The Insider/Outsider Problem in the Study of Religion*. London: Cassell, 1999.

Otto, Rudolf, *The Idea of the Holy*. London: Oxford University Press, 1923.

Pals, Daniel L., *Eight Theories of Religion*. New York: Oxford University Press, 2006.

Van der Leeuw, Gerardus, *Religion in Essence and Manifestation*. London: Allen & Unwin, 1938.

TIMELINE OF WORLD RELIGIONS

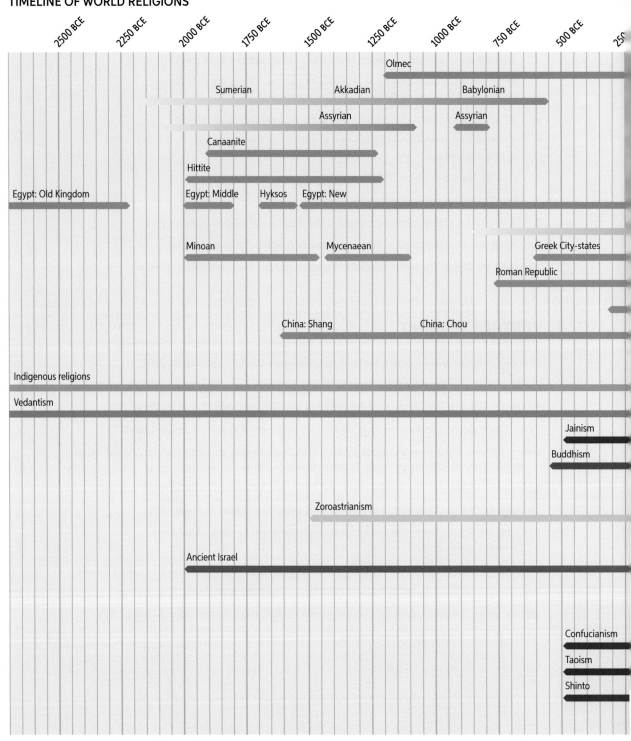

| | 2500 BCE | 2250 BCE | 2000 BCE | 1750 BCE | 1500 BCE | 1250 BCE | 1000 BCE | 750 BCE | 500 BCE | 25(|

Olmec

Sumerian · Akkadian · Babylonian

Assyrian · Assyrian

Canaanite

Hittite

Egypt: Old Kingdom · Egypt: Middle · Hyksos · Egypt: New

Minoan · Mycenaean

Greek City-states

Roman Republic

China: Shang · China: Chou

Indigenous religions

Vedantism

Jainism

Buddhism

Zoroastrianism

Ancient Israel

Confucianism

Taoism

Shinto

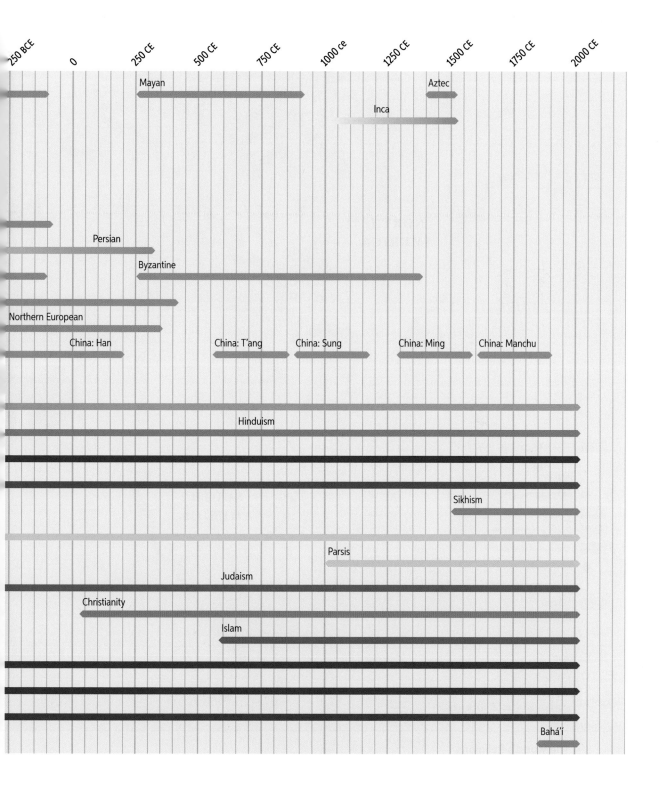

250 BCE · 0 · 250 CE · 500 CE · 750 CE · 1000 CE · 1250 CE · 1500 CE · 1750 CE · 2000 CE

Mayan
Aztec
Inca

Persian
Byzantine
Northern European
China: Han · China: T'ang · China: Sung · China: Ming · China: Manchu

Hinduism

Sikhism

Parsis
Judaism
Christianity
Islam

Bahá'í

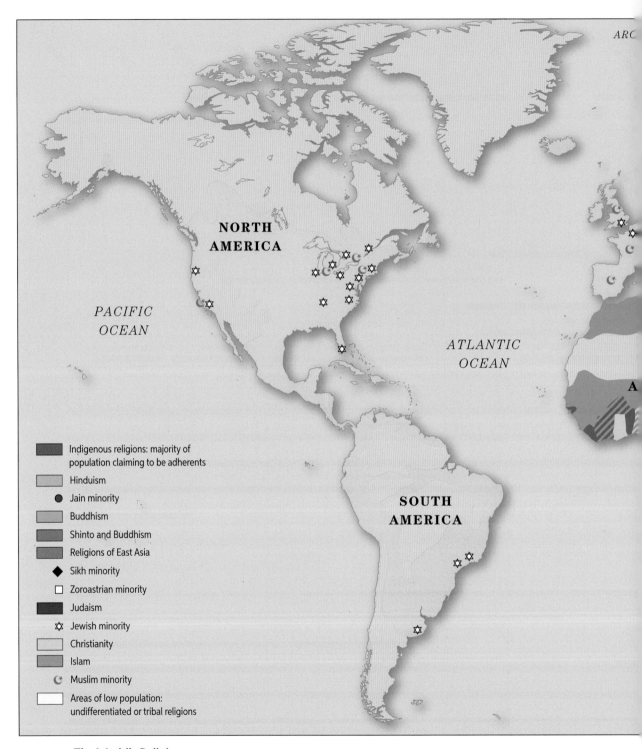

The World's Religions

A BRIEF INTRODUCTION TO JUDAISM

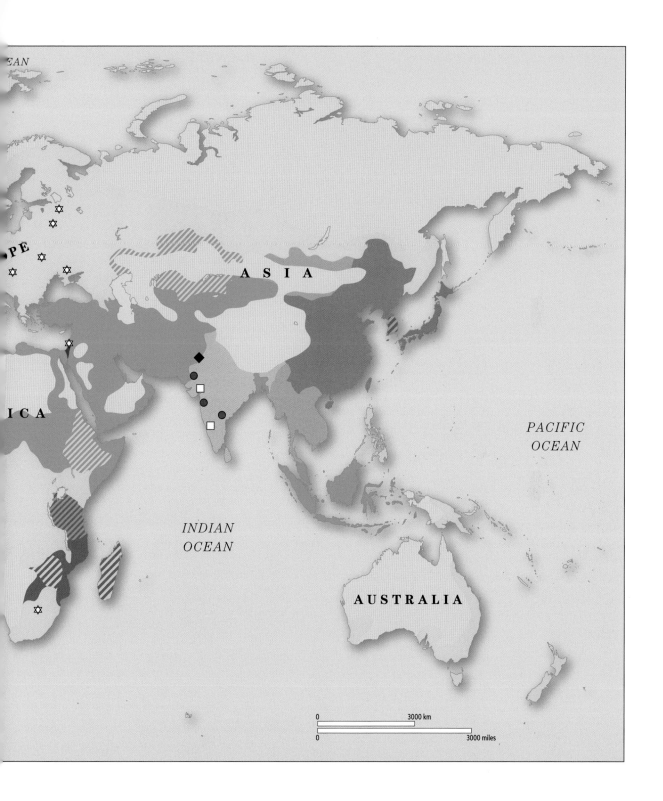

PART 2
JUDAISM

SUMMARY

More than any other world religion, Judaism can be thought of as the religion of a particular people – or indeed as *being* that people, rather than their religion. In part, this goes back to the shared, though disputed, story of national origin transmitted to us by scripture. According to this tradition, the people of Israel are bound by a covenant as God's elect to fulfil his obligations, in return for their special status. This tradition is central to the religion today: Judaism's most popular festivals, such as Passover and *Hanukkah*, commemorate key events from this version of the community's past. The religion of the ancient Judeans, based around the maintenance of the covenant through sacrificial rites, in time gave way to the rabbinic tradition, centred upon the synagogue, serving as a place of prayer, praise, and study.

The diaspora that followed the destruction of the Temple at Jerusalem in 70 CE carried Judaism across much of the Middle East, North Africa, and Europe. During the medieval period, many Jews – especially those in Muslim lands – made significant contributions to the arts and sciences, while those living in Christendom were frequently subjected to persecution and changing royal whim. By the twentieth century, though, Jewish communities formed part of the fabric of many European states. Reform of Judaism's tradition formed one distinct strand of the European Enlightenment, and the increasing separation of church and state at this time provided a framework into which Judaism could comfortably fit. More recently of a variety of schools of thought has emerged within Judaism, maintaining different approaches to doctrine and worship, and sometimes differing over how to respond to the changes and challenges of the secular world.

Much of recent Jewish history is overshadowed by the Nazi Holocaust, and for many the memory of this event highlights the importance Jewish traditions and of the community itself. Since 1948, the state of Israel has been a centre for this community and home – along with many other countries – to the diverse schools of thought that together make it up.

CHAPTER 9

A Historical Overview

Rabbinic Judaism today sees itself as a direct development from the time of Moses, the giver of the Torah, more than 3000 years ago. To understand the developing beliefs and practices of Judaism, we need to know something of the social and political events that affected Jewish communities. We also need to observe the ideas of their neighbours in order to understand the influence of the cultures with which they came into contact. Greek thought, Christianity, Islam, medieval philosophy, and charismatic movements have all affected the intellectual activity and popular customs of Judaism.

EXILE AND AFTER

The story of the early development of Judaism is much debated. The commonly accepted narrative, largely based on the polemical biblical texts of Ezra and Nehemiah — which actually refer to 'people of Israel' rather than 'Jews' — has been important for the later development of Jewish self-understanding, but is not necessarily founded in historical reality.

This popular story of Judaism begins in the late sixth century BCE, when the Persian Empire was dominant in the Middle East. In 586 BCE, Nebuchadnezzar II, King of the

I was glad when they said to me,

'Let us go to the house of the Lord!'

Our feet have been standing within your gates, O Jerusalem!

Jerusalem, built as a city which is bound firmly together,

to which the tribes go up,

the tribes of the Lord,

as was decreed for Israel,

to give thanks to the name of the Lord.

There thrones for judgment were set,

the thrones of the house of David. Pray for the peace of Jerusalem!

'May they prosper who love you!

Peace be within your walls,

and security within your towers!"

For my brethren and companions' sake

I will say, 'Peace be within you!'

For the sake of the house of the Lord our God,

I will seek your good.

Psalm 122, Old Testament, Revised Standard Version

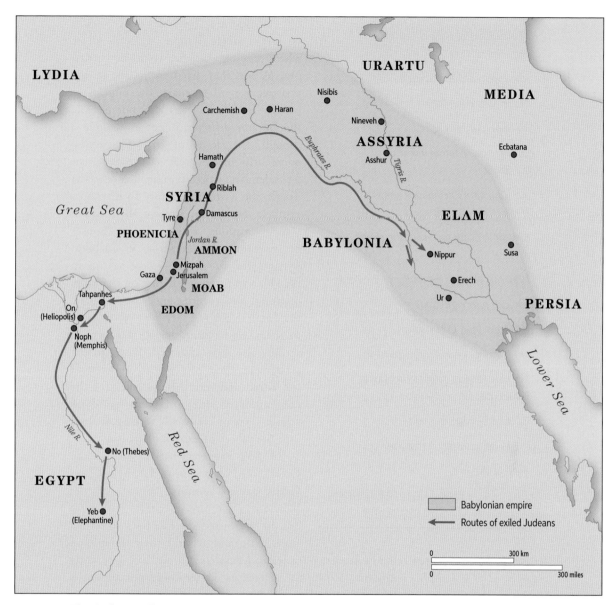

The Judean Exiles, c. 560 BCE

neo-Babylonian Empire, destroyed Jerusalem, and many its people were taken captive to Babylon, along with much of the population of Judea. In both Babylon and Egypt there were now communities of people who still considered themselves Judeans — consisting largely of mercenary soldiers and of prisoners of war and their families — some of whom were agents of the ruling power, and for that reason privileged. In Egypt, where this caused much resentment, the Judeans remained separate, following the religion and customs they brought with them.

> By the rivers of Babylon we sat and wept
>
> when we remembered Zion.
>
> There on the poplars
>
> we hung our harps,
>
> for there our captors asked us for songs,
>
> our tormentors demanded songs of joy;
>
> they said, 'Sing us one of the songs of Zion!'
>
> How can we sing the songs of the Lord
>
> while in a foreign land?
>
> If I forget you, O Jerusalem,
>
> may my right hand forget its skill.
>
> May my tongue cling to the roof of my mouth
>
> if I do not remember you,
>
> if I do not consider Jerusalem
>
> my highest joy.
>
> Psalm 137:1–6, Old Testament,
> New International Version

The Judeans believed there should be just a single Temple, the only place where religious sacrifice could be carried out. While they lived in Judah, it was possible for all to make the pilgrimage to this Temple in Jerusalem; but in exile this became difficult, if not impossible – though the Jews of the Dispersion apparently made great efforts to visit Jerusalem and worship in obedience to the Torah, the written teaching. To meet this obstacle, and in an attempt to maintain some continuity with the past, houses of assembly – *beitei knesset* in Hebrew, 'synagogues' in Greek – were set up in Babylon, and prayer, singing or chanting, teaching, and reading and discussion of the Torah – but not sacrifice – took place in them. Some time during this period, scribes also first appeared. Based in the synagogue, their role was to understand the Torah and interpret its rules for the contemporary situation. This 'guild of scholars' seems eventually to have evolved into the rabbis of rabbinic Judaism.

In 539 the army of Cyrus II, 'the Great', of Persia captured Babylon, and Cyrus gained nominal control of the Babylonian Empire. According to Ezra 1:3, he permitted the Hebrews to return from exile and rebuild their Temple in Jerusalem. When Hebrew religious leaders returned to Jerusalem, the city was apparently established as a Temple community, led by the priests, as Cyrus would not allow the restoration of the monarchy. According to Ezra/Nehemiah, a strict separation between Judean – 'Jews' – and non-Judean in Judah was enforced by the Hebrews' leaders, Ezra and Nehemiah, a separation apparently marked by circumcision, observance of *Shabbat* – the Jewish Sabbath – and of the Sabbatical year, recognition of the Torah (the first five books of Jewish scripture), and obligations to the Temple in Jerusalem. Rigorists also required that marriage arrangements should be made only between Judeans.

A BRIEF INTRODUCTION TO JUDAISM

THE HELLENISTIC KINGDOMS

After Alexander the Great won the Battle of Issus in 333 BCE, an era of prosperity commenced in the region. Cities founded on the Greek pattern grew rapidly, with Alexandria becoming the leading city in Egypt within a few years of its foundation. The Judean community there was substantial, and Greek — rather than Aramaic — became their language. People even tried to look Greek! The Greek language was the medium by which Greek ideas, attitudes, and ways of reasoning were passed on. People who could read Greek — especially those living in Alexandria — might have had an opportunity to read the great Greek philosophers in the original. But it seems Greek-speaking Jews were not drawn away from their customs as much as some feared, and still visited Jerusalem to celebrate the festivals in the Temple.

After the death of Alexander, his empire broke up into smaller units, principally the kingdoms of Macedonia, Egypt, and the Seleucids. When the Parthian Empire rose to power in the third century BCE, the Seleucid Kingdom, which had included Babylon, was gradually reduced to only the Syrian region, and Babylon came under Parthian control. The Jews remaining in Babylon were now cut off from other Jewish communities, and Aramaic remained their language, adding a linguistic barrier to that of politics. The Jewish communities of Babylon and of the Greek-influenced, or 'Hellenized', kingdoms inevitably developed differently, though they were united by a common scripture and emphasis on Jerusalem and its Temple, where priests were leaders, and the high priest politically and economically powerful.

TENSION AND REVOLT

In 191–190 BCE the Romans, turning their eyes towards the East, defeated King Antiochus III of Syria; it was probably prisoners of war from this conflict who founded the Jewish community in Rome. Jews also settled in Antioch, Syria, and in Asia Minor, modern Turkey. The Romans exacted tribute from Antiochus, which meant increased taxes. Consequently tension grew between rich and poor in Jerusalem and Judah, which — along with the political and cultural divisions between those for and against Hellenism — made for a volatile situation.

The explosion came during the reign of Antiochus IV Epiphanes (175–164). When the Jews resisted his nominee for the high priesthood, he sent troops to sack Jerusalem, established pagan practices in the Temple, and attacked the Jewish religion. Some Jews submitted, but those who adhered to the Torah, especially the *Hasidim* — 'The Pious' — suffered greatly. Eventually there was full-scale revolt, led by the Maccabee family, and — against the odds — Judas Maccabeus came to terms with the Syrians in 165 BCE, marched on Jerusalem, and ritually cleansed the desecrated Temple. This victory, and the reconsecration of the Temple, is celebrated today in the Festival of Lights, or *Hanukkah*.

The Maccabee family now began a line of rulers — the Hasmonean dynasty — many of whom, ironically, became typical Hellenistic despots. However they won a measure of freedom for the Jewish realm before the Romans, under Pompey, annexed Judea in 63 BCE.

UNDER THE ROMAN EMPIRE

Judea now became a vassal of Rome. The current Hasmonean king was confirmed as the nation's leader and high priest, but the Romans refused to recognize him as king.

In 40 BCE, following a Parthian invasion of Syria and Judea, Rome gave Herod (c. 73–4 BCE), son of Antipater the Idumean, the title 'king of the Jews'. Although his personal life was disastrous, the country prospered under his rule, and Herod 'the Great' is remembered as a builder of cities such as Sebaste and Caesarea, of fortresses such as Masada and Herodium, of palaces, theatres, and amphitheatres, and of the Jewish Temple in Jerusalem. Those who opposed Rome and Hellenism hated and opposed him.

During the Roman period Jewish hopes rose for a messiah – a king of David's line, for some, a priest-king – who would rescue his people from the Romans and restore the Judean state. There were several revolts in Judea during the time of Herod and his successors, and 'prophets' attracted large followings. The most serious threat to the Jews came during the reign of the Emperor Caligula (37–41 CE), who demanded that all his subjects worship him, and ordered a statue of himself as Zeus to be placed in the Jerusalem Temple.

Ptolomaic Empire

Seleucid Empire

○ City with Jewish population

THE TEMPLE DESTROYED

Judea became increasingly unsettled. In the coastal cities, conflict between Greeks and Jews was constant, and tension mounted between the Roman governors and the people. Finally in 66 CE the Jews rose in revolt against Rome, but initial success was followed by crushing defeat, Jerusalem was taken, and its Temple destroyed in 70 CE.

The destruction of the Temple was decisive for the future of Judaism. The Temple, the priesthood, and the council – the Sanhedrin – were finished. No longer could Jerusalem act as a unifying force within Judaism, the focus of pilgrimage. Jewish communities now became just one group within larger communities; although distinct, they were inevitably affected by the culture of the city or nation in which they found themselves.

HELLENISTIC JUDAISM

The life of the ordinary Jew in Greek-speaking areas centred on the synagogue, where worship and practical matters of community life were conducted. Strangers were lodged,

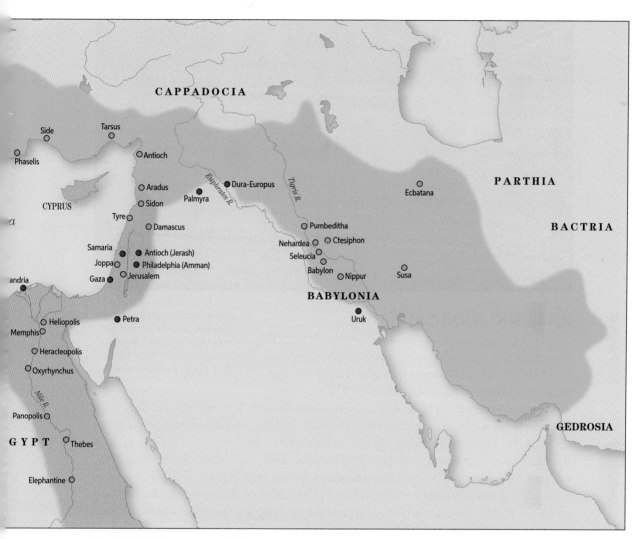

The Jewish Diaspora c. 240 BCE

the poor helped, discipline enforced, public gatherings held, and children taught in the synagogue. Visiting preachers might give a sermon, but the resident scholars probably did not. Authority was in the hands of the 'ruler of the synagogue'. Associated with the synagogue was the 'house of study' (*bet midrash*), where the Bible was studied and scholars could consult a library.

Some Hellenistic rabbis drew up rules of biblical interpretation. Philo of Alexandria (20 BCE–50 CE) attempted to explain the Bible from the point of view of Greek philosophy, presenting the great events of Israel's history as allegories of eternal truths and adopting the Stoic idea of Reason (*Logos*), which he called a 'second God', an intermediary between God and the world.

RABBINIC JUDAISM

A seemingly insignificant event provided a new direction for Judaism when Johanan ben Zakai (30–90 CE) founded a school at Jamnia, or Yavneh, Galilee, where

rabbi (master) became the formal title for teachers. Though Johanan may not have been a Pharisee, his successor, Gamaliel the Elder, was, and the school's ethos was essentially Pharisaic, the stance of emerging rabbinic Judaism. The school at Jamnia came to exercise the function of a council, and even adopted the name 'Sanhedrin'. Johanan fixed the calendar for Jews abroad – once the prerogative of the high priest – and Jews began to look to this council for advice and judgments. The rabbis of this early period are known as *Tanna* – plural *Tannaim*, 'teachers'. Their earliest surviving works are 'sayings' in the *Pirkei Avot*, sometimes known as the 'Ethics of the Fathers', and second-century written Hebrew versions of Jewish oral traditions known as the Mishnah.

Most other varieties of Judaism gradually died out. Jewish Christianity survived into the second century CE, although the rabbis tried hard to exclude Jewish Christians from the synagogues after about 90 CE. In the Greek world, Christians broke entirely with Judaism, often becoming anti-Jewish.

PERSECUTION

Jewish revolts against Roman rule continued widely and were brutally put down. The Judean revolt of 132 CE may have been ignited by the establishment of the new Roman city of Aelia Capitolina upon the ruins of Jerusalem; the Old City of present-day Jerusalem is the linear descendant of this Roman town. This revolt was led by Simon ben Kosiba, also known as Simon bar Kokhba – 'Son of a Star', who claimed to be the messiah, and who was supported by the greatest rabbinic scholar of the day, Rabbi Akiva ben Joseph (c. 40– c. 137 CE). But the uprising was hopeless, and the casualties inflicted on the Romans only made the final defeat more harsh.

The governors of Palestine – the name the Romans now gave the country – were now higher-ranking Romans than previously. Construction of Aelia Capitolina was completed, and Jews forbidden to enter the city. Galilee now became a centre of Jewish life, and several different towns in succession became the seat of the Jewish council. Judaism was not banned, but the circumcision of converts was forbidden, making conversion difficult, if not impossible.

PALESTINIAN PATRIARCHATE

Simeon ben Gamaliel II became president of the 'Great Sanhedrin' and first Palestinian Patriarch with – at least in theory – authority over all Jews of the Roman world. His son, Judah I, the Prince (b. 135) – also known as Rabbi HaQadosh – appears to have exercised considerable power. A noted scholar, during his time the Mishnah was codified and published. The Palestinian Patriarchate came to an end with the execution by the Romans of Gamaliel VI in 425, and the Sanhedrin was also dissolved as a result of Roman oppression.

The conversion of Constantine to Christianity in 313 was not auspicious for Jews. Although Judaism was never made illegal, life became difficult for Jews, as Jewish-Christian tensions grew. In Egypt, the Jewish community began to recover, though numbers were never as high as in earlier centuries. Greek culture was on the wane, and with it Hellenistic Judaism.

BABYLONIAN EXILARCHS

In Babylon, the ruler of the Jews of the Diaspora were known as an 'exilarch', or head of the exiles. This hereditary position was recognized by the state and, later, under Arab rule by the Muslims. But from the fifth century onward, relations between the Jews and the Persian authorities became difficult, and the Jews there welcomed the Arab conquerors. Similarly, in Palestine, the harshness of the Byzantine rule caused the Jews to look for help abroad, aiding the invading Persian forces in 614. However uprisings among the Jerusalem Jews in 617 were subdued by military force when the Byzantine army re-entered the city, and the Jews were once more expelled.

JUDAISM AND ISLAM

Islam arose and spread with extraordinary rapidity in the seventh and eight centuries CE. Muslim Arabs defeated the Byzantine army in 634, conquered Syria and Palestine, defeated Persia in 637, and Egypt soon after. Muslims invaded Spain in 711, and set up a Muslim state. Within a century, many Jews had come under Muslim rule. For most, living conditions improved considerably, and the Jews shared in the intellectual ferment of the Arab world. Arabs translated and studied the learning of Greece, Persia, China, and India, and drawing on these resources, Muslim and Jewish scholars made great advances in mathematics, astronomy, philosophy, chemistry, medicine, and philology. One of the greatest Jewish philosophers, Saadiah Gaon (882–942), grappled with the problem of 'faith and knowledge', discussing proofs of God's existence.

BABYLON: THE AGE OF THE GAONS

In Babylon, the authority and importance of the Gaons – the heads of the Babylonian academies – grew immensely after 600. The Gaons ensured that the Babylonian Talmud – documents compiled in the Babylonian academies between the third and fifth centuries – became accepted more widely. In the ninth century a gaonate was established in Palestine, and was recognized as authoritative by Jews in Spain, Egypt, and Italy. Under the Gaons collections of Talmudic laws were made, synagogue poetry written, prayer-books drawn up, and the text of the Bible was fixed and annotated. Most influential were the *Responsa* (Hebrew, *She'elot ve-Teshuvot* – questions and answers) – questions on matters of practice sent to the Gaons, debated in the academies, and answered in their name.

Variants from rabbinic Judaism arose. In eighth century Babylon, Anan ben David (c. 715–c. 795), and Karaite movement he possibly founded, rejected the Talmud and all forms of oral law, such as the Mishnah, taking a stand on the Bible only. It seemed the Karaites might divide the Jewish world, but the movement soon became merely a sect, which still survives today in small numbers.

SCHOLARSHIP IN SPAIN

Jews rose to influential positions at court in Spain, where 'Sephardic' Judaism developed, with its own synagogue rituals and a Spanish-Jewish dialect, Ladino. Solomon ibn Gabirol (c. 1021– c. 1058) attempted to reconcile Jewish thought with Neo-Platonism – which posits that God is separated from the world by a descending series of 'emanations' – which contributed to the development of the Jewish mystical tradition known as the Kabbalah (see below). Judah Halevi of Toledo (1085–1140) wrote a fictional dialogue between a Jewish scholar and the king of the Khazars – a Turkish tribe converted to Judaism – showing that philosophy could prove God's existence, but that revelation was then necessary to know more of him.

JEWS IN WESTERN EUROPE

From the mid-eleventh century Jewish scholars in the West became more important than the Gaons. The French scholar Rabbi Solomon ben Isaac (Shlomo Yitzhaki, 1040–1105), known, from his initials, as Rashi, produced standard commentaries on the Bible and Talmud. With additions by his successors, his commentaries are still printed in the Talmud.

In the eleventh century there was a shift in philosophical thought, as Aristotle supplanted Plato. Aristotle's science seemed to leave no room for religion, and Jewish scholars debated whether his philosophy could be reconciled with biblical religion. In Córdoba, Spain, the Rabbi Moshe ben Maimon (Moses Maimonides, 1135–1204) presented a code containing all the *halakhah* in his Mishneh Torah. Exiled from Spain to Egypt, he wrote in Arabic the great philosophical work *The Guide for the Perplexed*, discussing the difficulties Aristotle's philosophy presented for the believer. Although Judaism had been — and is — far more based on right behaviour — orthopraxis — than orthodoxy, Maimonides saw 'right belief' as of great importance, for which he was much criticized. Maimonides also drew up thirteen 'roots' of Judaism, the 'Thirteen Principles of the Faith'.

> *This God is one. He is not two nor more than two, but one. None of the things existing in the universe to which the term one is applied is like unto his unity.*
>
> Moses Maimonides,
> *Mishnah Torah*

THE RISE OF ANTI-SEMITISM

From the tenth century onwards, anti-Jewish sentiment and riots became common in France, and life in Christian Europe generally became difficult for Jews. The Crusading armies marching to the 'Holy Land' looted and slaughtered Jews as they went, and the capture of Jerusalem — hailed by Christendom as a great triumph — meant death for the Jews there. Many Jews regarded such death as martyrdom, the ultimate form of witness, or 'sanctification of the Name' (*kiddush haShem*), and some committed suicide rather than renouncing their faith. Jewish rules of conduct (*halakhah*) stated that in some situations death was preferable to the alternative — for instance to avoid idolatry, incest, or murder, or to 'sanctify the Name'.

In Europe, two vicious lies circulated: the 'blood libel' and the 'libel of desecration of the host'. The blood libel claimed Jews were guilty of ritual murder, using the blood of Christian children during Passover. The 'libel of desecration of the host' spuriously

THE THIRTEEN PRINCIPLES OF THE FAITH

- Belief in the existence of a creator and of providence
- Belief in his unity
- Belief in his incorporeality
- Belief in his eternity
- Belief that worship is due to him alone
- Belief in the words of the prophets
- Belief that Moses was the greatest of all the prophets
- Belief in the revelation of the Torah to Moses at Sinai
- Belief in the unchangeable nature of the revealed Law
- Belief that God is omniscient
- Belief in retribution in this world and in the hereafter
- Belief in the coming of the messiah
- Belief in the resurrection of the dead

JUDAISM TIMELINE

2000 BCE	1500 BCE	1000 BCE	500 BCE	0	500 CE	1000 CE	1500 CE	2000 CE

c. 1800 BCE Traditional date for Abraham, first Patriarch ◆

c. 1280 BCE Traditional date when Moses leads Exodus from Egypt ◆

c. 1000 BCE King David takes Jerusalem, makes it his capital ◆

c. 950 BCE King Solomon completes first Temple in Jerusalem ◆

922 BCE Northern kingdom separates on Solomon's death ◆

722 BCE Assyrians conquer Northern kingdom, disperse its people ◆

621 BCE Josiah centralizes worship at Jerusalem Temple ◆

586 BCE Babylonians conquer Jerusalem, exile leaders and people ◆

538 BCE Persians conquer Babylon, permit Hebrew exiles to return ◆

515 BCE Second Temple dedicated ◆

164 BCE Rededication of Jerusalem Temple after Maccabean revolt ◆

70 Romans besiege Jerusalem, destroy Herod's Temple ◆

c. 90 By tradition, canon of Hebrew scripture completed ◆

c. 200 The Mishnah of Rabbi Judah ha-Nasi completed ◆

c. 400 Palestinian Talmud completed ◆

c. 600 Babylonian Talmud completed ◆

882–942 Saadiah Gaon, Jewish philosopher, Babylonia ◀▶

1040–1105 Rashi, commentator on Bible and Talmud ◀▶

1135–1204 Maimonides, author of *The Guide of the Perplexed* ◀▶

1250–1305 Moses de Léon, author of *Zohar* ◆

1492 Jews expelled from Spain ◆

1520–23 Printed edition of Talmud published in Venice ◆

c. 1698–1759 Israel ben Eliezer, the *Baal Shem Tov*, in Poland ◀▶

1729–86 Moses Mendelssohn, pioneer of Reform in Germany ◆

1881 Pogroms in Russia spur Jewish westward emigration ◆

1889 Conservative Judaism separates from Reform in USA ◆

1897 Theodor Herzl and the first Zionist Congress ◆

1938 German synagogues vandalized ◆

1938–45 Holocaust (*Shoah*) – destruction of much of European Jewry by the Nazis ◆

1948 State of Israel established ◆

A BRIEF INTRODUCTION TO JUDAISM

THE KABBALAH

In the Kabbalah, God was known as the 'limitless' (*En Sof*), from whom came ten aspects of God (*Sefirot*), by which he is manifested and made known. These 'emanations' of God mediate between the *En Sof* and the world.

The most important work of the Kabbalah is the *Zohar*, attributed to Rabbi Simeon bar Yochai (Rashbi, first century CE), but in reality written in thirteenth-century Spain. The 'Talmud of Jewish mysticism', its final editor/author was probably Rabbi Moses de Léon (c. 1250–1305). Although the study of the Torah is still central in Kabbalah, the aim is to find hidden, secret meanings; the *Zohar* expounds the Torah by literal, allegorical meanings, but more importantly, by mystical insights. Astrology is also bound up in the *Zohar*: each day is influenced by one of the ten *Sefirot*.

After the Jews were expelled from Spain, the centre of Jewish mysticism became Safed, Galilee, where Rabbi Isaac Luria (1544–72) gave a new slant to the Kabbalah, using much erotic imagery, which greatly influenced later movements, such as Hasidism. In Luria's view, after the *En Sof* created the universe, he withdrew from it, leaving *Sefirot*, vessels that contain the 'divine light'. The last six *Sefirot* could not contain the light, and shattered. Some of them sank, trapping sparks of the divine light within them. This is the origin of evil; redemption will come when these sparks are returned to their source.

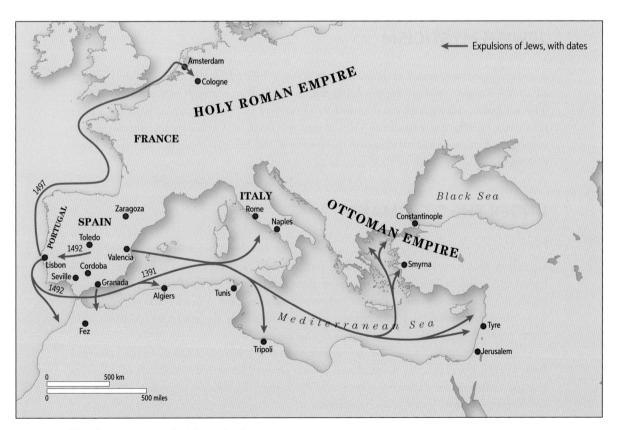

The Jews are expelled from Spain

claimed that Jews stole the host – the consecrated bread of the eucharist, believed to be the body of Christ – and stabbed or burned it, thus re-enacting the crucifixion of Jesus.

Jews entered England during the eleventh century, but were expelled in 1290, not to return until after 1650. Between 1290 and 1293, Jewish communities in southern Italy were almost wiped out and many forced conversions were made. The Jews were expelled from France in 1306, and massacres occurred in 1348. Jews were falsely accused of poisoning wells and causing the Black Death, a plague that killed off one third of the population of Europe in 1348. From Spain to Poland, Jews were persecuted and massacred.

In the twelfth century Christians attempted to recapture Spain from the Muslims. In response, the Muslim Almohades from North Africa pushed into Spain and, not showing their usual tolerance towards Jews, drove them northwards. Christian leaders at first welcomed these Jews. With other means of livelihood closed to them, many became moneylenders, since usury was forbidden for Christians. But tolerance did not last, and in Christian Spain attacks on Jews reached a peak in 1391. Many Jews professed conversion to Christianity, and were known by the insulting name of *Marranos* (swine). In 1492 Jews were offered the choice of converting or leaving; thousands fled to other parts of Europe and beyond, such as Safed in Galilee.

JEWISH MYSTICISM

Another important strand of Judaism is mysticism: belief in some kind of direct 'vision' of divine things, a way of experiencing things other than through our ordinary senses. The Kabbalah, a Jewish mystical tradition, developed in Spain, bringing together earlier traditions, such as ideas from the Talmud and the Book of Creation (*Sefer Yetsirot*), which emphasized the mystical meaning of the letters in the Hebrew alphabet and from Neo-Platonism a concept of how God related to the world.

UNDER THE OTTOMANS

During the sixteenth and seventeenth centuries, the Muslim Ottoman Empire was in the ascendant, capturing Palestine in 1515, Egypt in 1517, and expanding into Europe, until halted in Vienna in 1683. Most Jews now lived either in Christian Poland–Lithuania, or under the Muslim Ottoman Empire, where conditions were generally less difficult, but where they were still subject to arbitrary or capricious acts of the rulers. In Christian Italy, severe penalties were inflicted on the Jews in this period.

The Protestant Reformers on the whole favoured Jews, but Martin Luther changed from tolerance and defence to rabid anti-Jewish abuse. The rite of non-Sephardic Jews in Europe – especially in Germany – known as 'Ashkenazi' dates to the sixteenth century, and has its own German-Jewish dialect, Yiddish.

Anti-Jewish riots continued, but the authorities now more often protected the Jews, who were seen as useful for their money-lending and trading. In Ukraine and Poland many Jews were killed in massacres in 1648 and 1649, when Jewish leaders were seen by the peasantry to be economically and politically at one with the Polish overlords.

HOPE OF A MESSIAH

In the late seventeenth century a number of Jewish messianic movements arose, partly a product of the insecurity of Jewish life. The most important was centred on Shabbetai Zevi (1628–1716) and his prophet, Nathan of Gaza (1643–80), who called for repentance, strict ascetic practices, and mortification of the body – including fasting, bathing in freezing water, and constant prayer. Shabbetai was imprisoned in Gallipoli in 1665, and in 1666, under coercion, converted to Islam. His remaining followers were viewed with deep suspicion by the Jewish community, and the episode resulted in general disillusion with Messianism.

HASIDISM

Eighteenth century Poland saw the rise of Hasidism, a popular movement that gave hope and excitement to people who were frightened and deprived, with its emphasis on emotion and devotion. The movement focused on the individual and direct experience of the divine, and was thus accessible to ordinary labourers, who could not afford the long hours of study required by rabbinical Judaism. The key figure in the growth of Hasidism was Israel ben Eliezer (1700–60), known as the Baal Shem Tov, 'Master of the Good Name'; a dynamic, charismatic figure, widely known as a miracle worker, whose teaching contained much from the Kabbalah, especially the *Zohar*.

Many legends are told about Baal Shem Tov, and much popular belief – indeed superstition – was caught up into the movement. But at the core was a passionate devotion to God, expressed in ecstatic prayer, singing, and dancing. From outside, Hasidic life may seem a narrow existence, but it is sustained by Hasidic 'joy' – a genuine religious 'high'.

The leaders of Hasidic groups were more gurus than rabbi-like scholars. The leader, *rebbe*, or *zaddiq*, is a man who lives the life of devotion, and acts as intermediary between his followers and God. His word is absolute: his followers leave their families to be with him, and even contest for a share of the food he has touched. There are a number of different branches of Hasidism today. Women played a much more prominent role in the beginnings of the movement than they do today. Generally, Hasidism is a man's world; Hasidic women lead separate lives.

The Hasidic movement met strong opposition from the Jewish establishment, with something of a class struggle, as *rebbes* replaced the rich and learned. One of the most hostile opponents was the Gaon of Vilna, Elijah ben Solomon (1720–97), an ascetic intellectual who excoriated Hasidism. The Hasidic Jews were sometimes excluded from the community – and even betrayed to hostile authorities. Influenced by Shneur Zalman of Liadi (1745–1812), his Chabad branch of Hasidic Judaism was reconciled to Talmudic study and thus accepted by the wider Jewish community.

GO WEST

From the early seventeenth century, Jews gradually began to move from Poland and the Ottoman Empire into the cities of the West. There was a growing recognition of the value of Jewish commercial activity, and Jews began to be associated with the more developed social and economic systems. During the nineteenth century, large numbers of Jews migrated to America. Judaism remained the target for abuse and oppression, but there was a growing tolerance. During the nineteenth century equal rights were eventually obtained in many countries, though often with great difficulty.

JEWISH ENLIGHTENMENT

The 'Jewish enlightenment', *Haskalah*, pointed to another new direction within Judaism. Its founder, Moses Mendelssohn (1729–86), advocated the separation of church and state, so that religious bodies should not be able to compel, only persuade. He emphasized the universal principles of religion within Judaism, and translated the Torah into German. After his death, this movement, now led by Leopold Zunz (1794–1886), became more radical, rejecting the Talmud and traditional ideas – even the idea of revelation.

> All things that are, are in God, and must be conceived through God, and therefore God is the cause of the things which are in himself. This is the first point. Further, no substance can be granted outside God, that is, nothing which is outside God exists in itself; which was the second point. Therefore God is the immanent, but not the transcendent, cause of all things.
>
> Baruch Spinoza, *The Ethics* (1677).

At the beginning of the nineteenth century, emancipation in France, Italy, and Germany allowed Jews to leave the ghetto and – as a result of *Haskalah* – develop reformed Judaism. Emancipation also aided the assimilation of Jews – sometimes even their cultural disappearance, when Jews merged through marriage into the surrounding society. After emancipation, the lifestyle of many Jews began more closely to resemble that of their non-Jewish fellow citizens.

The dark counterpoint to increased tolerance was anti-Semitism, based on a belief in the 'soul' of a people; a contrast was drawn between the 'Semitic' nature of Jews and that of the 'Aryan' or 'Slavonic'. Strongly anti-Semitic movements were promoted in Germany and France from the 1880s, the direct consequence of which was the destruction between 1939 and 1945 of six million people in the Holocaust, simply because they were Jewish. European Jewry almost ceased to exist, and one-third of world Jewry was killed.

GEOFFREY COWLING
REVISED BY TIM DOWLEY

CHAPTER 10

Sacred Writings

The texts of Judaism have long been central to its life and culture, as can be seen in many expressions. In the Torah, Deuteronomy 30:14, we read: '... the word is very near to you; it is in your mouth and in your heart for you to observe' (literally: for you to do). Psalms and wisdom also hint at the centrality of texts. For example, the psalmist proclaims: 'I treasure your word in my heart, so that I may not sin against you ... Your word is a lamp to my feet and a light to my path' (Psalm 119:11, 105).

Reading the Torah scroll using a *yad* ('hand'), a Jewish ritual pointer, to ensure the parchment is not touched by hand.

In the reign of King Josiah (c. 639–609 BCE; see 2 Kings 22–23), it is the discovery of the 'book of the Law' (an early form of Torah) that inspires Josiah's reforms. From the late biblical period until classical rabbinic Judaism, the scribe, from the copyist to the 'maker' of scrolls or books, has been regarded as something of a hero, often on a par with a sage and, eventually, a *reb* or rabbi.

A Jewish legend reflects the sacredness of texts. It tells of a Roman soldier who defaced a Torah scroll in the first century CE, and whom the authorities put to death to avoid insurrection. Since the destruction of the Temple in 70 CE, and the final revolt against Roman authorities (132–35 CE), sacrifice and pilgrimage to the Temple was replaced with the study of Scripture and other sacred texts, prayer, and works of piety.

The study of texts made Judaism a portable tradition. Jews of the diaspora, or exile, were able to worship God anywhere, and the study of sacred texts could also be done anywhere. Today, the sacredness of texts is expressed in other ways too. Since the advent of printing, Jewish writers and publishers have been at the forefront of the book industry. Modern *halakhot* (observances) include stipulations about the proper treatment of books. Judaism has always exhibited a remarkable love of the word, of manuscripts, and of books.

There are three major textual traditions:

- Tanakh (Hebrew scriptures)
- Mishnah (tractates and regulations on the Law)
- Talmud (exposition of the Mishnah and Torah)

TANAKH

In Jewish practice and theology the term 'torah' is used in three senses:

- the first five books of the Scriptures, traditionally ascribed to Moses
- the whole of the Jewish Scriptures (written torah)
- ethical teaching of the rabbis (oral torah)

This article only uses the term in the first sense, referring to the first five books. In referring to the whole of Hebrew scripture, we use the term 'Tanakh', which derives from the tradition since late antiquity of dividing the Hebrew scriptures into three distinct sections.

> *There is one way to salvation: to go back to the sources of Judaism, to Bible, Talmud, and Midrash; to read, study, and comprehend them in order to live them ... the seekers after knowledge will go back to the ancient fountains of Judaism, Bible, and Talmud and the one effort will be to obtain the concept of life out of Judaism.*
>
> Samson Raphael Hirsch,
> *The Nineteen Letters on Judaism*
> (1836), transl. B. Drachman
> (New York: Feldheim, 1960).

Much debate surrounds how and why particular books came to be included in the Jewish canon, and in what order. The order is significant. For example, in the Jewish canon the Book of Ruth is in the Writings and belongs to a group of five books (the *megillot*) that are read cyclically at festival times, Ruth being read at harvest.

In Judaism the notion of canon itself has evolved over the centuries. From the earliest records, what mattered was the pragmatic nature of texts: which texts manage to speak with immediacy — beyond the context of their composition —to the ongoing life and identity of the faith community? Once identified, those texts are 'biblical'. These are texts that, for whatever reason, accrued existential value for the community who used them.

MISHNAH

The Mishnah is a collection of tractates consisting of *halakhot*, observances which cover every conceivable area of Jewish daily life and ritual purity. Its first tractate, the sayings of the fathers, *Pirqe Avot*, begins by laying down some principles for interpretation and for practice. The first verse sets the tone:

> *Moses received Torah from Sinai and passed it on to Joshua, and Joshua to the Elders, and the Elders to the Prophets; and the Prophets passed it on to the men of the Great Assembly. They said three things: 'Be careful in giving judgment, raise up many disciples, and make a fence around the Torah.'*

In other words, like Jewish writers after them, the authors of the Mishnah saw themselves as part of an unbroken chain of tradition. Jews who fulfilled the ordinances of the Mishnah would in turn be fulfilling the Torah, building a hedge around it in a mutually beneficial exchange: guard the Torah and it will guard you. From its inception (c. 200 CE), the Mishnah became the key reference for decision making among the diaspora Jews. However, within fifty to a hundred years large portions of it were thought to be terse and obscure, and an explanatory companion soon evolved.

TALMUD

The Talmud ('teaching'), a vast collection of writings containing the teaching of the rabbis, appeared in the rabbinic academies of diaspora Judaism out of the continuing debate about the significance and implementation of the Tanakh — especially the Torah — and the Mishnah, with tractates and groups of tractates gradually becoming authoritative through use.

There are two Talmuds: the Palestinian — also known as the Jerusalem Talmud — a record of discussion in the rabbinic schools of Galilee, especially Tiberias, during the fourth century CE; and the longer Babylonian Talmud, completed in the seventh or eighth century CE, recording the opinions of more than a thousand rabbis between 200 and 650 CE. The Babylonian Talmud was used by Jews living in the Muslim Empire, whilst the Palestinian Talmud was influential in Italy and Egypt.

These lengthy collections — the Babylonian Talmud amounts around 4 million words — contain many kinds of literature. The scholar Solomon Schechter (1847–1915) described the Talmud as 'a work too varied, too disconnected, too divergent in its elements, to be concisely defined at all, or even approximately to be described within the limits of an English sentence'. For this reason, we have to be careful about taking any particular opinion in the Talmud as 'the teaching of Judaism'. The Talmud records many views, so it is necessary to discover who said what, how authoritative it was, whether it was accepted by the later authorities, and what later commentaries said about it.

The range of topics the Talmud covers is astounding. Hyam Maccoby's anthology of the Talmud, *The Day God Laughed*, organizes its material into such categories as: Enjoying Nature, Against Asceticism, Physical Beauty, Eating and Drinking, Rejoicing, Studying; Tall Stories, The Value of Argument, Arguing for Pleasure, Arguing with God, and Privy Etiquette. The Talmud is at pains to blur any distinction between holy and profane, and is not concerned with answers. It is far more concerned with questions — and the process of answering them. One of its most celebrated passages captures this:

On that day, Rabbi Eliezer put forward all the arguments in the world, but the sages did not accept them.

Finally, he said to them, 'If the halakhah *is according to me, let that carob-tree prove it.'*

He pointed to a nearby carob-tree, which then moved from its place a hundred cubits, some say, four hundred cubits. They said to him, 'One cannot bring a proof from the moving of a carob-tree.' ...
[Two more miracles were performed by Rabbi Eliezer in a bid to have his argument accepted.]

Then said Rabbi Eliezer to the Sages, 'If the halakhah *is according to me, may a proof come from heaven.'*

Then a heavenly voice went forth, and said, 'What have you to do with Rabbi Eliezer? The halakhah *is according to him in every place.'*

Then Rabbi Joshua rose up on his feet, and said, 'It is not in the heavens.'
[Deuteronomy 30:12 – he goes on to explain that since the Torah has already been given on Sinai, we do not need to pay attention to a heavenly voice.]

Rabbi Nathan met the prophet Elijah. He asked him, 'What was the Holy One, blessed be He, doing in that hour?'

Said Elijah, 'He was laughing, and saying, "My children have defeated me, my children have defeated me."'

Bava Metsia 59b

In other words, God's children are grown up enough to argue with him; for the rabbi, it is even a responsibility. In this sense, the Talmud captures something essential, not just of the historical period and contexts it emerges from, but also of the ongoing life of Judaism: God is in the argument, and he may well be found in the delight of vigorous human discourse.

TEXTUAL BALANCE

In some ways, for modern Judaism the Tanakh is not the most important text. In matters of practice, the texts of classical rabbinic Judaism, of its subsequent commentators – such as the biblical *Targums* (paraphrases) and medieval texts such as the *Mishneh Torah* ('Copy of the Torah') of Maimonides, and commentaries by Rashi and Abraham ibn Ezra – and of a whole range of popular prayer books and guides to Jewish life, including the *Zohar* and *Shulhan Arukh* (c. 1565) – are often the first port of call. Yet for the composers of the Mishnah, Tanakh was the foundation not just of the laws being composed, but of life itself; and for the Talmud, Mishnah and Tanakh were foundational.

Judaism's sacred texts, then, can be envisaged as concentric circles: The innermost three circles are the Tanakh, at the very centre, Torah, followed by *Nevi'im* (the prophets), and *Ketuvim* (the writings). After that come Mishnah, Talmud, and *Midrash* ('commentary') – the ongoing tradition of commentary and critique, a potentially never-ending circle that includes all texts that manage to become, in some way, of existential value to the Jewish community.

ERIC S. CHRISTIANSON

DIVISIONS OF THE HEBREW SCRIPTURES

Torah
Genesis, Exodus, Leviticus, Numbers, Deuteronomy

Nevi'im (Prophets)
Former: Joshua, Judges, Samuel, Kings
Latter: major: Isaiah, Jeremiah, Ezekiel
Minor: the book of the twelve: Hosea, Joel, Amos, Obadiah, Jonah, Micah, Nahum, Habakkuk,
Zephaniah, Haggai, Zechariah, Malachi

Ketuvim (Writings)
Psalms, Proverbs, Job, Song of Songs, Ruth, Lamentations, Ecclesiastes, Esther, Daniel, Ezra, Nehemiah, Chronicles

CHAPTER 11

Beliefs

In the Hebrew Bible, the Israelites experienced God as the Lord of history. The most uncompromising expression of his unity is the *Shema* prayer: 'Hear, O Israel, the Lord our God is one Lord' (Deuteronomy 6:4–9). According to Scripture, the universe owes its existence to the one God, the creator of heaven and earth, and since all human beings are created in his image, all men and women are brothers and sisters. Thus, the belief in one God implies, for the Jewish faith, that there is one humanity and one world.

GOD AND CREATION

For the Jewish people, God is conceived as the transcendent creator of the universe; that is to say, God is distinct from that which he has created, above and beyond the world. He is 'wholly other' than anything that is not God. Unlike creation, God is uncreated and does not depend upon anything for his existence. Thus he is described as forming heaven and earth:

> In the beginning God created the heavens and the earth. The earth was without
> form and void, and darkness was upon the face of the deep; and the Spirit of
> God was moving over the face of the waters.
>
> Genesis 1:1–2

Throughout the Bible this theme of divine transcendence is repeatedly affirmed. The prophet Isaiah proclaims:

> Have you not known? Have you not heard? Has it not been told you from the
> beginning? Have you not understood from the foundations of the earth? It is he
> who sits above the circle of the earth, and its inhabitants are like grasshoppers;
> who stretches out the heavens like a curtain and spreads them like a tent to
> dwell in.
>
> Isaiah 40: 21–2

Despite this view of God as remote from his creation, he is also viewed as actively involved in the cosmos. In the Bible, the belief that he is always omnipresent is repeatedly stressed. In the rabbinic period, Jewish scholars formulated the doctrine of the *Shekhinah* to denote the divine presence. As the indwelling presence of God, the *Shekhinah* is compared to light. Thus the Midrash paraphrases Numbers 6:25, 'The Lord make his face to shine upon you, and be gracious to you': 'May he give thee of the light of the *Shekhinah*'. In the Middle Ages the doctrine of the *Shekhinah* was further elaborated: according to Saadiah Gaon, the *Shekhinah* is identical with the glory of God, and serves as an intermediary between God and human beings during the prophetic encounter. Judah Halevi of Toledo argued in his *Kuzari* that it is the *Shekhinah* rather than God himself who appears to prophets.

Some feminists today see the *Shekhinah* as a way for women to connect spiritually to the divine, distinct from the normalized male attribute of God that occurs in many Jewish contexts.

TIME AND ETERNITY

The Hebrew Bible also depicts God as having neither beginning nor end, a teaching that was elaborated by the rabbis. According to the Talmud, there is an unbridgeable gap between God and humans:

> Come and see! The measure of the Holy One, blessed be he, is unlike the measure of flesh and blood. The things fashioned by a creature of flesh and blood outlast him; the Holy One, blessed be he, outlasts the things he has fashioned.

God's eternal reign is similarly affirmed in midrashic literature. Yet the rabbis discouraged speculation about the nature of eternity. The Mishnah states:

> Whoever reflects on four things, it were better for him that he had not come into the world: What is above? What is beneath? What is before? and What is after?

> Whither shall I go from thy Spirit?
>
> Or whither shall I flee from thy presence?
>
> If I ascend to heaven, thou art there!
>
> If I make my bed in Sheol, thou art there!
>
> If I take the wings of the morning
>
> and dwell in the uttermost parts of the sea,
>
> even there thy hand shall lead me,
>
> and thy right hand shall hold me.
>
> Psalms 139:7–12,
> Old Testament,
> Revised Standard Version

Despite such teaching, in the Middle Ages Jewish theologians debated this issue. In his *Guide for the Perplexed* Maimonides argued that time itself was part of creation; when God is described as existing before the creation of the universe, the 'time' should not be understood in its normal sense. This concept was developed by Joseph Albo in his *Ikkarim* (fifteenth century), where he argues that the concepts of priority and perpetuity can only be applied to God in a negative sense. That is, when God is described as being 'before' or 'after' some period, this only means that he was not non-existent before or after that time. However, terms indicating a time-span cannot be applied to God himself.

According to other Jewish thinkers, God is outside time altogether: he does not live in the present, have a past, or look forward to the future, but lives in the 'Eternal Now'. Hence, God is experiencing every moment in the past and future history of the created world simultaneously and eternally. What for us are fleeting moments rushing by are, for God, a huge tapestry, of which he sees every part continually.

OMNIPOTENCE AND OMNISCIENCE

Allied to this is the Jewish conviction that God is all-powerful and all-knowing. From biblical times the belief in God's omnipotence has been a central feature of the faith. Thus in Genesis, when Abraham's wife Sarah expressed astonishment at the suggestion that she should have a child at the age of ninety, she was criticized. Similarly, when Jerusalem was threatened by the Chaldeans, God declared: 'Behold, I am the Lord, the God of all flesh; is anything too hard for me?' (Jeremiah 32:27).

In the Middle Ages, however, Jewish thinkers wrestled with the concept of divine omnipotence. Maimonides, for example, argues in his *Guide for the Perplexed* that, although God is all-powerful, there are certain actions that he cannot perform because they are logically impossible:

Modern statue of Moses Maimonides, Rabbi Moshe ben Maimon (1135–1204), in Córdoba, Spain.

> *That which is impossible has a permanent and constant property, which is not the result of some agent, and cannot in any way change, and consequently we do not ascribe to God the power of doing what is impossible.*

Regarding God's omniscience, the Bible proclaims:

> *The Lord looks down from heaven, he sees all the sons of men … he who fashions the hearts of them all, and observes all their deeds.*
>
> Psalms 33:13, 15

Following the biblical view, rabbinic Judaism asserted that God's knowledge is not limited by space and time. Rather, nothing is hidden from him. Further, the rabbis declared that God's foreknowledge of events does not deprive human beings of free will. Thus, in the Mishnah, the second-century sage Akiva declares: 'All is foreseen, but freedom of choice is given.' In his *Guide for the Perplexed*, Maimonides claims that God knows all things before they occur. Nonetheless, human beings are unable to comprehend the nature of God's knowledge because it is of a different order from theirs. Similarly, it is impossible to understand how divine foreknowledge is compatible with free will.

THE ELECTION AND MISSION OF ISRAEL

The Bible asserts that God controls and guides the universe. The Hebrew term for such divine action is *hashgahah*, derived from Psalm 33:14: 'From where he sits enthroned he looks forth on all the inhabitants of the earth.' Such a view implies that the dispensation of a wise and benevolent providence is found everywhere: all events are ultimately foreordained by God. Such a notion was developed in rabbinic literature, where God is depicted as the judge of the world, who provides for the destiny of individuals as well as nations on the basis of their actions.

Jews further affirm that God chose the Jews as his special people:

> *For you are a people holy to the Lord your God: the Lord your God has chosen you to be a people for his own possession out of all the peoples that are on the face of the earth.*

> Deuteronomy 7:6

Through its election, Israel has been given a historic mission to bear divine truth to humanity. God's choice of Israel thus carries with it numerous responsibilities:

> *For I have chosen him, that he may charge his children and his household after him to keep the way of the Lord by doing righteousness and justice.*

> Genesis 18:19

THE TORAH

To accomplish this task, God revealed both the oral Torah and the written Torah to Moses on Mount Sinai. As Maimonides explains:

> *The Torah was revealed from Heaven. This implies our belief that the whole of the Torah found in our hands this day is the Torah that was handed down by Moses, and that it is all of divine origin. By this I mean that the whole of the Torah came unto him from before God in a manner which is metaphorically*

called 'speaking'; but the real nature of that communication is unknown to everybody except to Moses.

In rabbinic literature, a distinction is drawn between the revelation of the Pentateuch – the first five books of the Bible, and Torah in the narrow sense – and the prophetic writings. Such a distinction is frequently expressed within Judaism: the Torah was given directly by God, whereas the prophetic books were given by means of prophecy. The remaining books of the Bible were conveyed by means of the Holy Spirit rather than through prophecy. According to the rabbis, the expositions and elaborations of the written Law were also revealed by God to Moses on Mount Sinai, subsequently passed from generation to generation, and through this process additional legislation was incorporated, a process referred to as 'the oral Torah'. Thus traditional Judaism affirms that God's revelation is twofold and binding for all time.

> *Before the mountains were brought forth,*
>
> *or ever thou hadst formed the earth and the world,*
>
> *from everlasting to everlasting thou art God.*
>
> Psalm 90:2, Old Testament, Revised Standard Version

According to tradition, God revealed 613 commandments to Moses. These *mitzvot* are recorded in the Five Books of Moses and classified in two major categories:
- statutes concerned with ritual performances, char acterized as obligations between human beings and God;
- judgments consisting of ritual laws that would have been adopted by society even if they had not been decreed by God.

All these laws, together with their expansion in rabbinic sources such as the Mishnah and Talmud, are binding on Jewry for all time.

Rabbinic Judaism teaches that there are two tendencies in every person: the good inclination (*yetzer ha-tov*) and the evil inclination (*yetzer ha-ra*). The former urges individuals to do what is right, whereas the latter encourages sinful acts. At all times a person is to be on guard against the assaults of the *yetzer ha-ra*.

ESCHATOLOGY

Eschatology is teaching about the 'last things', such as the end of time, the afterlife, heaven, and hell. Traditional Judaism asserts that, at the end of time, God will send the Messiah to redeem his people and usher in the messianic age. In Scripture, such a figure is depicted in various ways, and as time passed the rabbis elaborated the themes found in the Bible and Jewish literature of the Second Temple period. In the midrashim and the Talmud they formulated an elaborate eschatological scheme, divided into various stages.

First there will be the time of the messianic redemption. According to the Babylonian Talmud, the messianic age will take place on earth after a period of decline and calamity, and will result in the complete fulfilment of every human wish. Peace will reign on earth; Jerusalem will be rebuilt; and at the close of this era the dead will be resurrected and joined with their souls, and a final judgment will come upon all humankind. Those who are judged righteous will enter heaven (*Gan Eden*), whereas those deemed wicked will be condemned to everlasting punishment in hell (*Gehinnom*).

However, 'when the Messiah comes' is also a colloquial way of saying 'never', and modern Judaism has become increasingly eschatology-neutral, particularly as a result of disillusion following such messianic disappointments of Bar-Kochba and Sabbati Zevi.

CHANGING BELIEFS IN MODERN TIMES

From biblical times Jews have subscribed to a wide range of beliefs about the nature of God and his activity in the world. In modern times, these have been increasingly called into question. In the nineteenth century, reformers sought to reinterpret this belief system for modern Jews. In their view, it no longer made sense to believe in the coming of the messiah and the eschatological scheme as outlined in rabbinic sources. Subsequent movements, such as Reconstructionist and Humanistic Judaism, rejected the supernaturalism of the past, and called for a radical revision of Jewish theology for the contemporary age. In more recent times, the Holocaust has raised fundamental questions about belief in a supernatural God who watches over his chosen people. Today there is widespread uncertainty in the Jewish world about the central tenets of the faith.

DAN COHN-SHERBOK

THE COVENANT

At the heart of the Jewish religion lies a covenant between God and the people. Unlike a testament, a covenant involves a personal response on the side of the second party to make it effective. Unlike a contract, it is not a mutually negotiated affair but is offered unilaterally by one side to the other. Yet it does provide rights and obligations to both parties – which is why, for instance, Jewish protest theology is usually grounded in a covenantal framework.

The covenants we are concerned with are between God and humankind, especially Israel. But investigation of civil treaties from the adjacent Hittite culture of the fifteenth and fourteenth centuries BCE provides interesting insights. These treaties – between king and people – always included three elements:

- a historical prologue, describing the deeds of the maker of the treaty;
- a list of obligations binding the lesser of the two parties;
- a list of punishments and rewards.

The Jewish covenants generally reproduce this pattern: they are grounded in divinely ordered events; they contain a set of stipulations; and they conclude with a list of 'woes and blessings'.

God's chosen people

The first covenant referred to in the Jewish scriptures is between God and Noah (Genesis 9:8–17), the basis for which lies in God's preservation of Noah and his family during the flood. Through Noah, a promise is made to humankind and the animal world that this disaster will never be repeated. The promise has its sign – the rainbow – which is to act as a reminder, both to God and all living creatures, of this undertaking.

The covenant with Noah provides the basis for the later, more specialized, commitment to Israel, the first of which is the covenant between God and the great patriarch of Israel, Abraham. God promises to make Abraham the ancestor of a great nation (Genesis 12:1–7),

and to give him and his descendants the land of Israel (Genesis 13:14–18). This covenant (Genesis chapters 15 and 17) begins with a historical introduction, stating God is the one who brought Abraham out from Ur of the Chaldees (in modern Iraq), and then outlines obligations about living righteously and justly, which are elaborated in later books. Circumcision becomes the sign of this covenant.

More than 600 years later, the Abrahamic covenant is reaffirmed and extended at Mount Sinai, with all the people who have come out of Egypt (Exodus chapters 19–20). This covenant recalls God's historical deliverance of them from Egypt, and the accompanying promise that Israel will be God's special possession among all the nations. There is a series of obligations in the form of the Ten Commandments, and the people's acceptance of their responsibilities is also indicated.

This covenant is again an expression of both God's grace and God's demands. Even the instructions are as much a gift as an obligation, for they show Israel how they may appropriately respond to God's choice of them. And, since God later maintains both sides of the covenant, even when elements within Israel fail to obey, the fact that the covenant is based on God's grace remains transparent.

All this is nowhere clearer than in the biblical book of Deuteronomy, which is presented as the record of Moses' farewell addresses to Israel, on the eve of their entry into the promised land. Deuteronomy 5 recounts the Sinai covenant, Deuteronomy 7 refers to the covenant with the patriarchs of Israel, and Deuteronomy 29 is a renewal of the covenant with the whole people. Throughout the book, insistence on God's continued, gracious maintenance of the covenant, despite Israel's failure to fulfil its conditions, is a prominent theme.

In the historical books a more specialized covenant is recorded – with David and his descendants and, associated with this, with the Levitical priesthood (1 Chronicles 17:7, 28:4). Here again there are the standard elements:

- the prologue reminds David it was God who turned him from a shepherd into a victorious king;
- the outlining of conditions indicates that God's blessing is not automatically guaranteed (1 Chronicles 22:11);
- the promise tells of God's commitment to establish David's descendants upon the throne forever.

A renewed covenant

So naturally did the people take the covenant on which their nation was based, that, except for Hosea and Jeremiah, the great prophets rarely referred to the Sinai agreement. Only after the exile shattered Israel's confidence were the prophets less reticent about the covenant (Zechariah 9:11; Malachi 2:4), while the later

Inside one of the caves at Qumran, Israel, where some of the Dead Sea Scrolls were discovered.

historical writings also speak of significant covenant renewals (Ezra 9; Nehemiah 9).

Most significant in a number of these writings is the promise of a new covenant to replace the broken one for which Israel had been punished (see, for example, Jeremiah 31; Ezekiel 16). The new covenant will have its obligations inscribed on the wills of the people rather than exist merely as external obligations which the people must seek to observe. When this happens, Israel will receive back all they have lost – and more.

In the post-biblical writings, further changes in the understanding of the covenant take place. The idea of a new covenant either drops away altogether, or becomes simply a reiteration of the old one (Baruch 2:30). In the apocryphal writings the word for covenant refers, much more frequently than before, just to the obligations within it. This tends to push the Torah into a more prominent position and the covenant in a more contractual direction. Meanwhile the covenant with the Fathers comes to be regarded as irrevocable, leading to the use of the term for the Jewish nation itself (Judith 9:13).

Jewish apocalyptic writings preserve the same emphasis, and the term for covenant is used more often than previously for its sign, circumcision (Jubilees 15:13–14). The Torah is now said to precede the covenant, moving into a position of greater prominence (Ecclesiasticus 24:6; 44:19).

Some of the documents discovered at Qumran and known as the Dead Sea Scrolls, as well as Jewish rabbinic writings maintain the same perspective. The former take up the idea of the new covenant made with its community, but this is essentially a reaffirmation of the old covenant. The rabbinic writings occasionally suggest God's covenant with Israel rests upon their obedience as much as God's free choice.

Robert Banks

CHAPTER 12

Family and Society

According to Orthodox Jewish law, a Jew is one born of a Jewish mother, although it is possible to become a Jew by conversion. On the eighth day after his birth, a Jewish boy will be circumcised, a religious rite performed by a *mohel*, a trained and registered circumciser. When he is circumcised, the boy receives the Hebrew name which will be used at his *Bar-Mitzvah*, at his wedding, and on his gravestone.

During his early years, his mother is responsible for his religious education. As soon as he can speak, the boy is taught the words of the *Shema*. At about the age of five, he is sent to a synagogue religion class which is held after school on weekdays and also on Sunday mornings. One of the main activities of the class is to learn Hebrew and study the sacred books. For a girl, it is also important to learn how to keep a Jewish home. Increasingly in the Orthodox world, girls are also taught to study Torah, though not Talmud.

BAR-MITZVAH

At the age of thirteen, a boy becomes *Bar-Mitzvah*, 'son of the commandment'; on the *Shabbat* after his birthday he reads for the first time from the scroll of the Torah during the synagogue service. After the service, there is usually a party for family and friends. After this, he is regarded as a responsible person, is expected to fulfil all the duties of a Jew, and may count as one of the ten who are required to make a quorum for public prayer (*minyan*). A Jewish girl comes of age at twelve, and is considered to be *Bat-Mitzvah* 'daughter of the commandment'. It is increasingly the custom to hold a ceremony to mark this occasion.

PRAYER

A devout Jewish man prays three times a day – morning, afternoon, and evening – either in his home or in the synagogue. When he prays, he covers his head with an ordinary hat or a skull-cap (*yarmelka,* or *kippah*). In the morning he wears a prayer-shawl (*tallit*), which has tassels or fringes at the four corners in obedience to a command found in the Torah.

On weekdays he may also put on phylacteries (*tephillin*), black leather boxes containing four passages of scripture – Exodus 13:1–10 and 11–16; Deuteronomy 6:4–9 and 11:13–21 – strapped to the forehead and left upper-arm.

While Orthodox women are not obligated to time-bound *mitzvot*, or to wear prayer-shawls or lay *tephillin*, they are also strongly encouraged to pray, at least an abbreviated form of the morning and evening prayers. In other branches of Judaism, women may take on the full obligations of daily prayer, including *tallit* and *tephillin*.

When he goes out, the Orthodox Jew may continue to cover his head, as a mark of reverence towards God, in whose presence all life is lived. By the front door, both women and men pass the *mezuzah*, and touch it to remind themselves of their obligation to God. The *mezuzah* consists of a tiny scroll of parchment on which are written in Hebrew the opening paragraphs of the *Shema*: Deuteronomy 6:4–9 and 11:13–21. The scroll is housed in a wooden or metal container, and fixed to the upper part of the right-hand doorpost of the front door. A similar *mezuzah* is fixed to the doorpost of every room in the house.

KOSHER FOOD

It is the duty of a traditional Jewish housewife to safeguard the religious purity of the home, and one of her many responsibilities is to ensure the food eaten there is *kosher* – fit or clean according to Jewish dietary laws. Meat and dairy products must not be served at the same meal: if meat is eaten, there can be no butter on bread, or milk in coffee. To avoid any possibility of mixing meat with milk, the traditional housewife uses two sets of dishes, one of which is only used for meat, the other only for milk foods. She may also use two bowls for washing-up and two sets of tea-towels. In *kosher* hotels, there are two separate kitchens.

Only certain kinds of meat, listed in Leviticus 11 and Deuteronomy 14, may be eaten in a Jewish home. Lamb, beef, and chicken are among those permitted; pork and shellfish among those that are not. The animals must be slaughtered by a trained and ordained *shochet*, who follows carefully prescribed regulations that cause the blood to drain quickly from the body and ensure the creature the minimum of pain. After the animal is slaughtered, the meat must be soaked in cold water and salted, to remove all the remaining blood.

Jewish people vary a great deal in their observance of these dietary laws. Some do not observe them at all, while some abstain from food that is expressly forbidden, but are not so particular about the details of keeping a *kosher* kitchen. However, Orthodox Jews follow these regulations meticulously as an act of religious obedience, whereby the taking of food is sanctified, and the family table becomes an altar. Before each meal, a traditional blessing is recited, and though this may vary according to the food that is being eaten, the most common words are, 'Blessed art thou, O Lord our God, King of the universe, who brings forth bread from the earth.'

A Jewish boy celebrates his Bar-Mitzvah at Jerusalem's Western Wall, Israel. Both the rabbi and the boy have *tephillin* strapped to their forehead, and the boy is wearing a cardboard *kippah*.

SHABBAT

Shabbat is considered to be the most important of all the Jewish religious festivals. It commemorates both the creation of the world, and the deliverance of the people of Israel from Egypt. It has played a significant role in the preservation of Judaism, and is a day with a special atmosphere of joy and peace. As such, it is thought of as a foretaste of the age to come.

The beginning of the *Shabbat*, sunset on Friday evening, is marked by the lighting and blessing of the *Shabbat* candles by the mother. The father attends synagogue, often with his children, and on his return blesses his children and praises his wife with the words of Proverbs chapter 31. The family then enjoys a *Shabbat* meal together, which begins with the blessing over bread and wine. The bread is a special plaited loaf called *challah*. Usually two loaves are used, in memory of the double-portion of manna that fell in the wilderness on the day before the *Shabbat*.

No work is permitted on the *Shabbat*, and Orthodox Jews have to be employed in occupations which allow them to be home before sunset every Friday throughout the year. This often means that they will be self-employed, work in a Jewish firm, or trade in Fridays and Saturdays for work on other evenings, Sundays and Christmas. No fires may be lit on the *Shabbat*, though a fire which was lit before the *Shabbat* may be left alight. Many install time-delay switches to avoid forms of work not permitted to Jews on the *Shabbat*. No long journeys may be undertaken on the *Shabbat*, though those on board ship do not have to get off. Orthodox Jews live within easy walking distance of their synagogue, since they must not drive on the *Shabbat* or use public transport.

Jewish skull-cap – *yarmelka* or *kippah* – prayer shawl – *tallit* – and Hebrew Torah.

These restrictions, far from being a burden, are seen by religious Jews as a means of releasing them from the ardours of the daily round. It is a day when they can rest completely from their ordinary work and be spiritually renewed.

At the close of the *Shabbat*, the family again gathers for a brief ceremony, called *havdalah*, 'separation'. Blessings, the '*Kiddush*', are recited over a cup of wine and a box of sweet spices, which speak of the fragrance of the *Shabbat* day, which it is hoped will be carried over into the new week.

MARRIAGE AND DIVORCE

In Judaism, marriage is considered to be a holy covenant between the bride and groom. Before the ceremony, the bridegroom signs the marriage document (*ketubbah*), in which he pledges himself to his bride. During the service the couple stand under an embroidered canopy supported by four poles (*chuppah*), which represents their future home. The ceremony ends with the breaking of a glass under the bridegroom's foot, a symbolic act thought by some to represent the idea that even times of great joy need to be balanced by moments of serious reflection. Others see it as a reminder of the destruction of the Temple of Jerusalem, a theme that constantly reappears in Hebrew prayers.

In the event of the breakdown of a marriage, the local community tries to reconcile husband and wife. If this is not possible, a *get*, or bill of divorce, may be issued by the Jewish religious court, if both partners agree. This document, written in Aramaic and signed by two witnesses, is handed by the husband to the wife and frees her from all marital obligations to him. In most countries, a civil divorce is required first, and the subsequent issuing of a *get* serves as a religious ratification of the divorce.

> Hear, O Israel: The LORD our God, the LORD is one. Love the LORD your God with all your heart and with all your soul and with all your strength. These commandments that I give you today are to be upon your hearts. Impress them on your children. Talk about them when you sit at home and when you walk along the road, when you lie down and when you get up. Tie them as symbols on your hands and bind them on your foreheads. Write them on the door-frames of your houses and on your gates.
>
> Deuteronomy 6:4–9, Old Testament, New International Version

DEATH AND RESURRECTION

The last words uttered by religious Jews when they are dying — or said on their behalf if they are too weak — are the words of the *Shema* which they first learned as children: 'Hear, O Israel, the Lord our God is one Lord…' At the funeral, close mourners make a small tear in their clothes, as a mark of grief. The funeral service, which is characterized by simplicity even among wealthy families,

A Jewish tombstone. Jews often place stones on the grave or tombstone, though the origin of this tradition is unclear. Possibly it is a symbolic act to show someone has visited the tomb, and the deceased is not forgotten.

A BRIEF INTRODUCTION TO JUDAISM

is arranged as soon as possible — preferably within twenty-four hours of death. No prayers for the dead are offered, but *kaddish*, a prayer of praise to God, is recited in their memory. It is the particular responsibility of children to say *kaddish* on in the memory of deceased parents.

After the funeral, close relatives return home for a week of private mourning, a period known as *shivah*, or the seven days, during which those who have been bereaved sit on low stools, or even on the floor. On the anniversary of the parent's death, the children light a memorial candle and recite the *kaddish* at the end of the synagogue service.

The idea of life after death can be traced back within Judaism at least 2000 years, and is expressed in Maimonides' 'Thirteen Principles of the Faith': 'I believe with perfect faith that there will be a resurrection of the dead at a time when it shall please the Creator.' Yet Judaism is concerned primarily with this life rather than the next, and with obeying the Law of God in the present rather than speculating about the future.

DAVID HARLEY

CHAPTER 13

Worship and Festivals

 An annual cycle of worship and festivals gives Judaism its distinctive form. There is a major or minor festival almost every month of the year. Beginning with *Rosh Hashanah*, New Year's Day, on the first day of *Tishrei*, and proceeding to the period of penitence that begins in the twelfth month, *Elul*, Jews are able to express and celebrate their identity through the regular re-enactment of stories that explore life's meaning and purpose. High and low points of the Jewish story are remembered year by year.

THE HEART OF JUDAISM

Maimonides' 'Thirteen Principles of the Faith' help define Judaism. They were not intended to become a creed — indeed, Judaism is based much more upon practice than belief — and can be summarized in the three great themes that underpin the Jewish religion: creation, revelation, and redemption.

At the heart of Judaism is the profound idea that human beings can bring God into the world through their everyday actions and interactions. Although Judaism acknowledges a huge distance between the infinity of God and the limitations of human beings, it believes we are called to be partners with God in the task of creation. This understanding of the divine–human relationship can be traced back to the Babylonian Talmud (*Shabbat* 10a, 119b, *Sanhedrin* 38a). The supreme moment of revelation was when the people received the commandments at Mount Sinai; hence, Jewish religious expression or worship occurs when *mitzvoth*, the commandments, are followed, as one practises *halakhah*, or 'walking in God's way'.

> *Judaism is a very practical and also a very joyful religion. 'Happy are we! How good is our lot! How pleasant is our destiny! How beautiful our heritage! Happy are we who, early and late, evening and morning, twice each day declare: Hear O Israel, the Lord is our God, the Lord is One!'*
>
> *The Jewish Prayer Book*, extract from the Morning Service.

HOME AND SYNAGOGUE

The object of greatest religious importance in Judaism is a scroll of the Law, a *Sefer* Torah. It is a moving moment when the Torah scroll is taken out of its protective ark in the synagogue during the course of a service of worship and held up before the people. The synagogue is important as a meeting place, a focus for prayer, and house of study. But it is not the only significant place of worship, in the sense in which a mosque or a church may be; Jews often refer to the synagogue simply as *shul*, school.

The home is the focus of many of the most central aspects of Jewish religious life, such as *Shabbat*, the festivals, and the dietary laws, as well as education across the generations. Every effort is made to involve children in the celebration of the major festivals. It is a child who asks the questions concerning the special night at the *Seder* celebration during *Pesach*, Passover. It is children who enjoy drowning out the sound of Haman's name whenever it is mentioned during the reading of the book of Esther at Purim. It is children who are given the best places in front of the lights of the *menorah*, candelabrum, at the festival of *Hanukkah*.

THREE PILGRIMAGE FESTIVALS

Three of the most popular biblical festivals are known as 'pilgrimage' festivals, since they recall the three annual occasions when Jews made the journey to worship in Jerusalem when the Temple played a central role in Jewish life. These are the eight-day festival of *Pesach* (Passover), *Shavuot* (Pentecost), and *Sukkot* (Tabernacles), also an eight-day festival. Together, they form an annual re-enactment of the special events that forged the relationship between the Jews and their God.

- *Pesach* (15–21/22 *Nisan*) remembers the Exodus from Egypt under the leadership of Moses, and celebrates the passage from slavery to freedom. The highlight is the first evening, with the observance of the *Seder*. Around the table in the home, Jews relive the story, often reading from the *Haggadah*, 'telling', the order of the Seder, and reflect how it must have felt to be a slave in Egypt (Exodus 13:8).
- *Shavuot* (6 *Sivan*) marked the bringing of the first fruits in the days of the Temple, and celebrates the giving of the Torah by God to Moses on Mount Sinai.
- *Sukkot* (15–20 *Tishrei*) commemorates the time when God protected the people in the desert.

In many ways, the story of the Exodus from Egypt did not end with Moses gaining freedom for a small group of people centuries ago. The theme of Passover gives a context

> The three Pilgrim festivals have in common the theme of joy in God's presence: 'And you shall rejoice on your festivals' (Deuteronomy 16:14–16) … The festive joy is traditionally expressed in feasting with meat and drink, and with the purchase of new garments for the women. It is a joy which is only complete when allied with concern for the needy; as the verse continues, 'with … the strangers, orphans and widows among you.'
>
> Rabbi Norman Solomon

SEDER MEAL

Through the ritual and symbolism of the *Seder* meal, Jews tell the story of how their ancestors left Egypt. The foods placed upon the often beautifully decorated *Seder* plate are symbolic and comprise: three wafers of unleavened bread, *matzot*, to symbolize the bread eaten by the Israelites when they left Egypt in a hurry (Exodus 12:39); bitter herbs, *maror*, to recall the experiences of slavery in Egypt (Exodus 1:14); a sweet paste, *haroset*, made from almonds, apples, and wine, to represent the mortar used for building in Egypt as slaves, and symbolize both the toils of slavery and the sweetness of redemption and freedom; a bowl of salt water to represent the bitter tears of slavery, with parsley used for dipping; a roasted bone, as a reminder of the Paschal lamb; and a roasted egg, as a reminder of the offering brought to the Temple for the festival with the Paschal lamb – these last two items being left on the *Seder* plate during the meal, and not eaten. It has also been the custom, since Rabbinic times, to drink four cups of wine during the *Seder* to represent the four stages of redemption, from the Exodus to the future coming of the messiah.

for exploration of the issues of freedom and slavery, and the accompanying themes of risk, choice, hope, disappointment, leadership, hardship, and sacrifice. Moses has inspired many people who have struggled to gain freedom from prejudice and oppression; issues of marginalization and possibilities for liberation in the contemporary world are often discussed during the *Seder* meal.

ROSH HASHANAH

The new year festival of *Rosh Hashanah* (1–2 *Tishrei*), as in many traditions, is a time for making resolutions about the future. However, for the Jews it is a serious occasion. A month earlier a forty-day period of penitence begins – the Ten Days of Awe, '*yamim noraim*' – and *Rosh Hashanah* marks the beginning of the last ten of these days. The foods eaten at the meal on New Year's Eve symbolize sweetness, blessings, and plenty. Bread is dipped into honey – rather than the usual salt – and the following prayer is said: 'May it be your will to renew for us a good and sweet year.' Prayers at the morning service the following day, which lasts up to six hours, focus on the characteristics of God as creator, king, and judge: the God who will show mercy and compassion to those who sincerely turn towards him, '*teshuva*'. The sounding of the ram's horn, '*shofar*', regularly through the service is literally a wake-up call to the people (see Amos 3:6).

From the Seder *liturgy*

This is the bread of affliction which our fathers ate in the land of Egypt.

Let all who are hungry come and eat.

Let all who are in want come and celebrate the Passover with us.

May it be God's will to redeem us from all trouble and from all servitude.

Next year at this season, may the whole house of Israel be free!

From the *Seder Haggadah, The Union Haggadah*, ed. The Central Council of American Rabbis, 1923.

YOM KIPPUR

The Day of Atonement, 'Yom Kippur' (10 Tishrei), is a fast day marking the end of the Ten Days of Awe, and is the holiest day in the Jewish liturgical year, when Jews solemnly review their record of behaviour and literally turn to face a new year. The whole day is spent in prayer for forgiveness and for a good year ahead, and for at least part of it synagogues are full to overflowing. Yom Kippur marks one of the most emotionally charged times of the Jewish year. The theme is return to God, 'teshuva' – a major religious theme within Judaism, involving a renewed commitment to walk in the right path. Kol Nidrei – a declaration in Aramaic – forms the beginning of the synagogue service, often sung to a moving melody, and sets the tone as the congregation gathers in awe.

Work is forbidden, as on Shabbat. There are five further prohibitions, 'innuyim', or forms of self-discipline, that apply during the Yom Kippur fast, and also the fast of Tisha b'Av, discussed below. Jews must abstain from eating and drinking, anointing with oils, sexual relations, washing for pleasure, and wearing leather shoes.

The Closing of the Gates, 'Ne'ilah', is the final service, as the fast ends, and emphasizes the importance of the last hour in which the gates of heaven remain open for a returning to God. Avina Malkenu, 'our father, our king', is chanted to express the congregation's commitment to the unity of God, followed by a final blow on the shofar.

A Jewish family in Israel celebrate Passover together with the Seder meal.

Festivals of Judaism

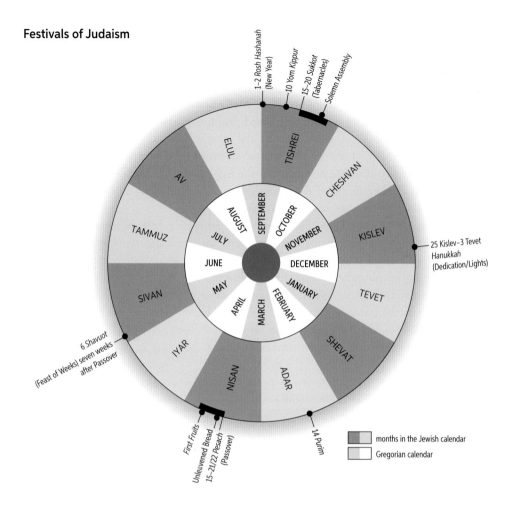

MINOR FESTIVALS

The most popular of the minor festivals are *Hanukkah* (25 *Kislev* – 2 *Tevet*), Purim (14 *Adar*), and the New Year for Trees, *Tu biShevat* (15 *Shevat*).

Hanukkah celebrates the rededication of the Temple in about 165 BCE, after its defilement by the Greeks. On each of the eight nights of the festival, a light is lit to commemorate the 'miracle of the oil'. The Hasmoneans, seeking to rededicate the Temple, could only find one cruse of oil, enough to keep the Temple *menorah* burning for a day – yet it lasted for eight. This is interpreted as symbolic of God's creative action in the world.

Between the destruction of the first Temple and the building of the second, many Jews were threatened with massacre by Haman's scheming with Ahasuerus, King of Persia, but Queen Esther and her uncle Mordechai were used by God to avert catastrophe. Purim celebrates this deliverance with parties and sending gifts of food to people in need, and the scroll of the book of Esther, *Megillah*, is read in the synagogue.

Judaism celebrates a new year for trees, *Tu biShevat*, a popular festival with the return to the land of Israel in modern times. In Israel it is marked by a school holiday and tree-planting ceremonies.

OTHER FAST DAYS

Of the other fast days the most important is 9 *Av* (*Tishah b'Av*), when the destruction of the two Temples, in 586 BCE and in 70 CE, is commemorated, as well as other tragedies of Jewish history. Reform Jews often use the day to commemorate the Holocaust.

On *Yom Kippur* and on *Tishah b'Av* people fast for twenty-five hours, instead of the twenty-four hours required for other fast days. Nothing is eaten or drunk during this time, unless there is a practical reason for not undertaking this discipline.

SECULAR JUDAISM

Many Jews who describe themselves as 'secular' nevertheless experience a sense of belonging to the wider Jewish community at times such as *Pesach* or *Yom Kippur*. Official Israeli holidays can also strengthen the links between communal identity and liturgy:

- Holocaust Day, *Yom HaShoah* (27 *Nisan*) remembers the Holocaust and the six million Jews who were murdered.
- Memorial Day, *Yom HaZikaron* (4 *Iyar*) remembers the soldiers killed defending the state of Israel.
- Independence Day, *Yom Ha-Atzma'ut* (5 *Iyar*) marks the anniversary of the founding of the State of Israel in 5708 (1948 CE).
- Jerusalem Day, *Yom Yerushalayim* (28 *Iyar*) commemorates the reunification of the city of Jerusalem in 5727, 1967 CE.
- The Israeli Declaration of Independence, proclaimed on 14 May 1948, is celebrated with social activities, in Israel and throughout the world, and special psalms and prayers are said in the synagogue, but is somewhat controversial, for both religious and political reasons.

LIZ RAMSEY

I AM A JEW

My paternal grandparents immigrated to Western Europe from Lithuania at the turn of the twentieth century to escape the effects of anti-Semitism and grinding poverty. My mother was born and brought up in Frankfurt-am-Main, Germany. She fled Germany at the end of June 1939, a refugee from Nazi persecution. She and her father were the only members of my maternal line to survive, the rest of the family are numbered among the millions of Jews murdered in the Holocaust. We live in a predominantly secular world, where religion and spiritual values are often assigned a very low priority. But, for me, my Jewish faith and family history have shaped and defined my identity. I attach great value to the traditions of democracy, freedom of speech, and equality before the law. I also feel a personal responsibility to contribute to building a better understanding and harmonious relations between the Jewish community and the non-Jewish majority among whom we live.

I also think I am incredibly lucky to be Jewish. I draw inspiration from the courage and fortitude with which my mother confronted both the difficulties of her childhood and the humiliation and poverty of being a refugee. No less inspiring is the example of friends who are Holocaust survivors. They are often the sole surviving members of their families, whose homes and communities were completely destroyed. Their suffering and loss is unimaginable. They were brutalized and terrorized solely because they

were born Jewish. Yet despite all this, so many of the survivors have chosen to renew and rebuild their lives firmly rooted in the Jewish faith and tradition into which they were born. This, for me, is proof of the eternal and enduring nature of their Jewish faith. The triumph of their humanity is truly inspiring.

Many of those murdered in the Holocaust were condemned in part because of the failure of so many countries, including the Western democracies, to take in Jewish refugees. So for me, and most Jews living in the diaspora (that is, Jews who live outside the borders of Israel), Israel represents a life insurance policy, a place of safety to which we can go if we feel we are once again endangered by anti-Semitism. Israel is, therefore, very important for the worldwide Jewish community. I have visited Jerusalem twice. It is at the heart and geographical centre of the Jewish world. Synagogues around the world are all built facing Jerusalem. The festival of *Hanukkah* and the fast days of *Tevet, Tammuz,* and *Av* have their origin in the sieges of Jerusalem and the desecration of the Temple. Each time I prayed at the *Kotel* – formerly known as the 'Western Wall' or 'Wailing Wall' – I sobbed uncontrollably.

For me Judaism is not just a religion, but a complete and distinctive way of life. It defines my relationship with God, my relationship with other people, Jewish and non-Jewish, and my obligations as a human being. The central and defining principal of Judaism is belief in a single God who is responsible for the creation of the universe and everything in it. The foundation of Judaism is the Torah, also known as the Five Books of Moses. I remember as a five-year-old schoolboy going after school to *cheder*, where I was taught to read Hebrew. At school I had to attend assembly each morning for Christian prayers, while at home, at the synagogue, and at *cheder* I was expected to follow Jewish religious practice and traditions. For a few years I found this mixture of Jewish and Christian teaching all very confusing, especially when one day at school I was beaten up because, according to my accuser, I had 'murdered little Lord Jesus'!

Every Jew is obliged to obey the law of the land, to do all they can to preserve human life, *pikuach nefesh*, and give to charity. This includes not only donations of money or goods, but acts of kindness, the promotion of education, and caring for the sick, needy, and elderly. On *Shabbat*, Jews are obliged to refrain from all forms of work: using machines, operating mechanical or electrical equipment, cooking, handling money, and travelling in a vehicle. For me, *Shabbat* is the one day of the week to which I always look forward: it is truly a day of physical and spiritual renewal.

David Arnold

Ancient chest, or "ark", for storing the Torah scrolls in a synagogue.

CHAPTER 14

The Holocaust

The term 'holocaust' originally referred to a burnt sacrifice offered to God in the ancient Jewish Temple. Today, 'Holocaust' is widely used to refer to the destruction of Jewry under the German Third Reich (1933–45), when bodies of many victims were burnt in crematoria. Many Jews consider the term *Shoah*, 'catastrophe', more appropriate, as it is devoid of religious connotations.

THE RISE OF NAZISM

At the end of World War I, Germany became a democratic republic, based on a constitution drafted in Weimar. The regime faced opposition from the extreme right and left, and during 1922 to 1923 there was massive economic inflation. An interlude of stability and intellectual and cultural development was followed by the Great Depression: over 6 million were unemployed between 1930 and 1933. Both the Communists and their fascist rivals, the NSDAP – *Nationalsozialistische Deutsche Arbeiterpartei*, the Nazi Party – gained considerable support. The Nazis, who linked Jews with Communism, were backed by leading industrialists. After several ineffectual conservative coalitions President Hindenburg (1847–1934) appointed Adolf Hitler as Chancellor on 30 January 1933.

Once in power, the Nazi Party suspended the constitution. In the course of 1933, other political parties were eliminated, strikes were outlawed, book burnings took place, and trade union leaders were imprisoned, along with dissident scientists, scholars, and artists. In 1934 the role of Hitler's elite security forces, the SS, was expanded, and led by Heinrich Himmler (1900–45) took over many of the functions of the police, as well as running the concentration camps.

THE EXTERMINATION OF JEWS

After Hindenburg's death, Hitler became the head of state. Civil servants and members of the armed forces were required to swear an oath of loyalty to him. Jewish academics

The Janusz Korczak Memorial, by Boris Saktsier, at the *Yad va-Shem* memorial to the victims of the Holocaust in Jerusalem, Israel.

lost their jobs, Jewish shops were boycotted, while the infamous Nuremberg Laws, 1935, criminalized sexual liaison between Jews and non-Jews, and prevented Jews from participating in civic life. In 1938 Jewish communal bodies were put under the control of the *Gestapo*, secret police, and Jews forced to register their property. 9 November 1938, *Kristallnacht*, the Nazis organized an onslaught against the Jewish population, killing, looting, and setting fire to homes, schools, shops, and 250 synagogues.

When the Nazis invaded Poland in 1939, in every conquered town and village the Germans forced Jews to hand over jewellery, clear rubble, carry heavy loads, and scrub floors and lavatories with their prayer shawls. Religious Jews had their beards and side-locks cut off with scissors or torn from their faces.

After the invasion of Russia in 1941, mobile task forces, *Einsatzgruppen* – murder squads of 500–900 men under the supervision of Reinhard Heydrich (1904–42) – began to slaughter Russian Jewry. Of the 4,500,000 Jews who lived in Soviet territory, more than half fled before the German invasion. Those who remained were concentrated in large cities, making it easier for Heydrich's troops to carry out their task. *Einsatzgruppen* moved in, rounded up Jews in market places, crowded them into trams, buses, and trucks and took them to woods where mass graves had been dug. They then machine-gunned them to death.

Other methods were also employed. Mobile gas vans were supplied to the *Einsatzgruppen*, and their killing operations were supplemented by the use of fixed centres, the death camps, at Chelmno and Auschwitz, in the Polish territories, and at Treblinka, Sobibor, Majdanek, and Belzec in the Polish 'General Government'. In September 1941 the first gassing took place in Auschwitz.

By September 1942 Germany had conquered most of Europe. But as the murder of Jews continued, resistance spread. The Jews of the White Russian town of Korzec set the ghetto on fire and a partisan group was formed. A former soldier in the Polish army escaped from a prison camp in Lublin with seventeen other Jews and formed a partisan group. In the Warsaw ghetto, the Jewish Fighting Organization prepared itself for action. When the Jews learned the ghetto was to be destroyed, they fought back. However, with vastly superior resources, the Germans prevailed: 7,000 Jews lost their lives in the fighting, and 30,000 were deported to Treblinka.

The murders continued without pause across Europe. By the summer of 1944, the last deportation took place, when more than 67,000 were deported from the Lodz ghetto to Birkenau. Most of these were selected for the gas chamber, but some were chosen for medical experimentation. By the end of World War II, more than 6 million Jews had lost their lives in the most terrible circumstances imaginable.

In the years since, the Jewish community has struggled with the religious perplexity of the Holocaust. Where was God at Jewry's time of dire need?

These terrible events are commemorated today on Holocaust Memorial Days, as well as in Holocaust Museums, such as *Yad va-Shem* in Israel, in an attempt to ensure that the murder of millions of Jews and others is not forgotten.

DAN COHN-SHERBOK

CHAPTER 15

Branches of Judaism

The majority of Jews throughout the world today are descendants either of the Sephardim or the Ashkenazim. Before being driven from Spain by the Inquisition in 1492, the Sephardim had been closely involved with the Muslim world, enabling them to develop a unique intellectual culture. Sephardic Jews – 'Sepharad' means Spain – created the Ladino language, a mix of Spanish and Hebrew.

The Ashkenazim came from central Europe, mainly Germany and France, and later moved to Poland and Russia. 'Ashkenaz' means the area inhabited by the Ashkenazim, who adhere to *minhag Ashkenaz* – a region that coincides with modern-day Germany, but also extends from France to the Pale of Settlement, the region within which Jews were allowed to reside by Imperial Russia. Ashkenazi Jews developed Yiddish – a mixture of Hebrew and medieval German – as their language and around it produced a culture rich in art, music, and literature. The difference in cultural background between the Ashkenazim and Sephardim is evident in Israel today, where each supports its own chief rabbi.

But the Jews are not a race, and Judaism is not an unchanging institution. Due to intermarriage, conversion, and dispersion among the nations, there has been a branching out over the centuries, and wide cultural differences between Jews have resulted. The difference between the black Falasha Jews of Ethiopia and the Indian Jews of Mexico, for instance, is immense.

In addition to these cultural groupings, several religious branches can be distinguished within Judaism today. Modern Judaism is rooted in rabbinic, or Talmudic, Judaism, and both evolved from biblical Judaism.

ORTHODOX JUDAISM

Orthodox Judaism regards itself as the only true Judaism. During the first half of the nineteenth century it developed into a well-defined movement, seeking to preserve traditional (classical) Judaism against the emerging Reform movement in East Europe.

Orthodox Jews are characterized by a 'Torah-true' approach to life, teaching that God personally and decisively revealed himself, in giving the Torah at Sinai, and that the words of the Torah are therefore divine and hence fully authoritative – the changeless revelation of God's eternal will. Every aspect of the Orthodox Jew's life is to be governed by the commandments (*mitzvot*). Jews are to study the Torah daily, and conform their lives to its propositions and rituals, including the strict rules of *Shabbat* observance, dietary laws, and prayer three times a day. In short, Orthodox Judaism is 'mitzvahcentric'.

At the start of the nineteenth century many East European Jews in rural areas lived in a close-knit community known as a *shtetl*, a stockaded, traditional culture shut off from the secular world. However, as large numbers started to emigrate to the United States, Orthodox leaders such as Rabbi Samson Hirsch (1808–88) encouraged Jews to involve themselves in the contemporary culture of the Western world, pursue secular university education, and develop philosophical thinking. Today, most Orthodox Jews believe adjustment to the modern world is legitimate, so long as it does not conflict with the teachings of the Torah.

Orthodox Jews maintain a high regard for the rabbi as teacher and interpreter of the Torah, and place a strong emphasis upon education, particularly day-schools where traditional learning can be acquired. Most Orthodox Jews are Zionist, supporting the state of Israel, and many hope for a personal messiah: an ideal man who will one day fully redeem Israel, although exactly what is meant by 'ideal' and 'redeem' is the subject of some debate. However few today would accept the divine authority of the Torah, the old test of 'Orthodoxy', and it is not uncommon for Jews to belong to both an Orthodox and a Progressive or Liberal synagogue. The term 'Orthodox' was originally used as a label for traditionalists opposed to radical change; now there are many shades of Orthodoxy, as the energy inspired by the Reform movement influences most Jewish groupings.

REFORM JUDAISM

Reform Judaism had its origins in Germany, where the Enlightenment of the eighteenth century stressed reason and progress. Emancipation in the following century opened the Jewish people to new freedoms, to equal rights as citizens, and to new opportunities to explore secular society. Jews quickly began to adapt to this new age, geared to change, growth, scientific inquiry, and critical evaluation. To meet this move away from Jewishness, Abraham Geiger (1810–74) and others declared that modern people could no longer accept the revelation of the Torah as factual and binding, and encouraged changes in ritual law and worship. Dietary laws were abandoned, prayers were translated from Hebrew into the vernacular, and synagogue worship was changed – the organ was introduced, services shortened, and the 'family pew' replaced segregation of the sexes. Some Jews even began to worship on Sunday rather than *Shabbat*.

In the USA, the Reform movement was led by Isaac Wise (1819–1900), who founded an organization of Reform congregations, and in 1875 set up the Hebrew Union College, the main seminary for training Reform rabbis. While Reform Judaism is one of the most progressive major branches of modern Judaism, active in the area of dialogue between faiths, the smaller Reconstructionist and Renewal movements are more radical in such areas as gender and political activism. Since the 1970s, Hebrew Union College has ordained women rabbis.

Liberal (Reform) Judaism[1] is still evolving – as revelation is seen to be a continuing process – and seeks to keep current with each new generation, using reason and experience to establish the relevance or truth of a proposition. Thus the ethical teachings of the prophets are emphasized rather than the ritual Law. Reform Judaism provides an individualized, non-authoritarian approach to religion; a law is observed, not because God said so, but because it is meaningful to modern religious experience.

Many Jews claim the Reform movement is now the most creative component within Judaism. With younger Jews no longer feeling that Judaism is defined by suffering and persecution, they are exploring the boundaries of cultural experience and convey a sense of expectancy for a new age of Judaism.

CONSERVATIVE JUDAISM

Many European Jews were uncomfortable with the radical changes introduced by Reform Judaism, and as a result Conservative Judaism arose at the end of the nineteenth century, emphasizing the historical elements of the Jewish tradition. As president of the newly-founded Jewish Theological Seminary, Solomon Schechter (1850–1915) led the movement in the USA, stressing commitment to tradition – with adjustments if necessary. Conservative Judaism thus has roots in Orthodoxy and Reform, and combines the ideals of both, preserving traditional Jewish practices, but holding that Jewish law can be reinterpreted in the light of modern views and trends – such as the findings of modern historical criticism.

Conservativism has maintained a strong emphasis on the people of Israel and modern Zionism. Laypeople have considerable influence: some congregations, for instance, permit the use of the organ, while others do not; some emphasize dietary laws, others do not. Conservative Judaism is possibly the largest single Jewish grouping in North America. In Israel and Britain, where it has been a more recent development, it is known by its Hebrew name, *Masorti*.

RECONSTRUCTIONIST JUDAISM

Reconstructionist Judaism is an outgrowth of Conservative Judaism, based on the work of the scholar Mordecai Kaplan (1881–1983), who stressed Judaism as an evolving culture, giving equal importance to religion, ethics, and culture. Reconstructionist Judaism doesn't fit neatly into the traditional/liberal, observant/non observant continuum. Although

---

1   In the UK, there is a difference between Liberal/Progressive Judaism, which is closer to American Reform Judaism, and Reform Judaism, which is somewhat closer to the American Conservative movement.

there are few Reconstructionist groups outside the United States and Israel, the movement has influenced Judaism, contributing to a reappraisal of basic concepts such as God, Israel, and Torah. Since its inception in the late 1960s, Reconstructionism has developed the use of inclusive language, encouraged women to be fully involved in liturgical practice, and accepted people with one Jewish parent as Jewish. Reconstructionists are actively involved in developing liberal Judaism in Israel.

THE HASIDIM

The Hasidim, founded by Baal Shem Tov, have many sects around the world, each led by its own *rebbe*. However, there is — and has been historically — much controversy over whether the Hasidim inappropriately substitute the judgment of the *rebbe* for the laws of Torah.

In some Hasidic groups the men have a distinctive style of dress, including black coats and hats, and wear ear-locks. They have a joyful form of worship, involving song and dance. In the United States, the Lubavitch and Satmar sects are especially influential. Some Hasidim are ultra-Orthodox, living in isolation from the Gentile world. The Renewal Movement, with roots in the 1960s counter-culture, attempts to reinvigorate Judaism, drawing on elements from Jewish mystic, Hasidic, musical, and meditative traditions, and has been criticised by some as 'New Age'.

HUMANISTIC JUDAISM

Humanistic Judaism began in 1965 with the rejection or reinterpretation of the beliefs of traditional Judaism. For example, supernatural beliefs are denied, and the Exodus from Egypt is seen as a myth. Humanistic Jewish worship is very different from traditional worship, and rarely uses the word 'God'. Unlike traditional Judaism, Humanistic Jews 'welcome into the Jewish people all men and women who sincerely desire to share Jewish experience regardless of their ancestry.' The principal institution of Humanistic Judaism is the International Federation of Secular Humanistic Jews.

ULTRA-ORTHODOX JUDAISM

The Haredim, or Ultra-Orthodox Jews, view the total separation of Judaism from the modern world as a religious obligation. Whereas Sephardic Haredim generally support Zionism and the State of Israel, many Ashkenazi Haredim oppose both.

> *We believe in the value of human reason and in the reality of the world which reason discloses. The natural universe stands on its own, requiring no supernatural intervention. We believe in the value of human existence and in the power of human beings to solve their problems both individually and collectively. Life should be directed to the satisfaction of human needs. Every person is entitled to life, dignity and freedom. We believe in the value of Jewish identity and in the survival of the Jewish people. Jewish history is a human story.*
>
> Proclamation stating the ideology and aims of Humanistic Judaism

RECENT DEVELOPMENTS

The collapse of the Soviet Union led to a rapid acceleration of Jewish immigration to Israel. Due to the earlier Soviet restriction of religious freedom, however, many of these immigrants came to Israel severely limited in their understanding and practice of Judaism. Unemployment, housing needs, and political unrest among Israelis and Palestinians created additional hardships associated with return to the Land.

The increased secularization of society has continued to threaten Jewish religious and community life through assimilation and intermarriage. To help counter these and other challenges, Chabad Lubavitch launched a successful programme of outreach towards unaffiliated Jews.

MARVIN WILSON
REVISED BY TIM DOWLEY

CHAPTER 16

Judaism in the Modern World

Jewish communities can be found in most parts of the modern world, which means there are great cultural and social variations as well as religious diversity within Judaism. Out of a worldwide total of around 13 million Jews the largest groupings live in Israel — 5,000,000 or 78.7 per cent of local population — and the USA — 5,700,000 or 2.1 per cent of local population. Although Jews account for no more than 0.25 per cent of the world's population, it would be hard to find another group of people who have had so much influence on the world in so many ways over such a long time. There is little sign of this influence lessening, in spite of the challenges facing Jewish survival. In the technological and scientific developments of the modern age, Jewish knowledge and expertise have a high profile, from medicine and genetic engineering to art and architecture. Jews are also prominent in the worlds of entertainment, law and politics. It is amazing how influence on this scale has been maintained despite the appalling loss of people and centres of learning that took place between 1933 and 1945.

WHO IS A JEW?

This question is hotly debated within contemporary Judaism. The Orthodox insistence that a Jew must be born of a Jewish mother — or convert according to Orthodox criteria — is largely disregarded by Reform Jews, but can lead to painful situations concerning identity and status for partners and children. The Reform view is that a person is a Jew if one parent is Jewish and that person is raised in a Jewish community. Moreover, conversion to Reform Judaism is a much simpler process. However, the term 'Judaism' does not only refer to a religion; more than fifty per cent of all Jews in Israel today call themselves 'secular', and half of the Jews in the USA do not belong to a synagogue or temple. Jews can be described as a 'nation' or 'people' — but the question of whether Judaism is a religion or ethnicity or peoplehood is complex and hotly debated.

> 'Lo alecha ha-mamlacha ligmor,' *says the Mishnah.*
>
> *'It is not incumbent on you to complete the work (of repairing the world), but neither are you free to evade it.'*
>
> Pirkei Avot 2:16

ISRAEL

Since its establishment in 1948, the state of Israel has been the focus of the Jewish world. In this tiny strip of land, only twelve miles wide in places, Jews from more than one hundred cultures mingle. All Jews, inside or outside Israel, feel an obligation to assess their relationship with Israel. Within Israel there are serious tensions between secular, Orthodox, and Ultra-Orthodox Jews concerning their attitudes to it. Some groups of Orthodox Jews do not support the existence of a Jewish state at all, and consider the militarism involved in preserving the state to be a contradiction of fundamental Jewish values.

The Zionist movement, dating back to Theodor Herzl (1860–1904), includes many supporters who prioritize the preservation of the Jewish people over the preservation of the Jewish religion. Herzl's dream was simply to establish a Jewish homeland after centuries of exile.

A common Israeli view, shared by many Jews in the diaspora, is that Israel needs to be strong in order to provide a safe haven for Jews all over the world, to provide a feeling of security and, perhaps even more importantly, hope for the future.

A minority fundamentalist group, *Gush Emunim*, 'Bloc of the Faithful', founded in 1974 in the wake of the

Interior of Eldridge Street Synagogue, Lower East Side, Manhattan, the oldest Eastern European synagogue in the USA.

Yom Kippur War, claims a divine right to the settlement of the West Bank, the Gaza Strip, and the Golan Heights — and sometimes as far as the Euphrates — as part of Israel.

JEWISH RELIGIOUS LIFE

Religious Jews pray and study Torah. They observe the dietary laws, keep the Sabbath and the festivals, and try to apply Jewish ethics in a global context of commerce and business. Jews are keen to observe religious regulations that emphasize the importance of the family and marriage. They are also aware of the responsibilities involved in being members of a community that is international as well as local, including praying together, providing welfare support, sharing in times of sadness and joy, and becoming involved in the cycle of rituals and festivals. In so doing, the religious Jew receives a glimpse of what heaven on earth might be like.

From the first century CE onwards, the rabbinic tradition bonded the Jewish people. Today there are more Jews studying in rabbinical seminaries than at any time since the great Babylonian academies. But following the rabbinic tradition is only one way of being Jewish.

Committed Jews remain faithful because the continuing story of Judaism depends on such commitment. Traditionally, Jews have shared a strong sense that there is a divine purpose for humanity, and that they have a special role in achieving it. The covenantal relationship between the Creator and creation, described in the Torah, means that together God and human beings may embark on the task of repairing or mending the world, *tikkun olam*.

Jews and Judaism have shown an amazing capacity to adapt to changing times and circumstances, while preserving the vital traditions central to the faith — a capacity closely linked to a strong emphasis on interpretation as well as revelation. For many Jews do not view revelation as something that happened solely once and for all in the distant past, but that there are different layers of meaning of Torah that can be rediscovered and interpreted in the light of contemporary contexts and needs.

> To be a Jew means first belonging to the group ... Judaism is an evolving religious civilization.
>
> Mordecai Kaplan

At the core of Jewish life is an immense store of moral energy. 'Social justice' is much the highest scoring factor that Jews in the United States give as relevant to what being Jewish involves. The restless drive to 'perfect the world under the sovereignty of God' remains after other practices have been abandoned. Judaism puts a high value on the dignity and responsibility of human beings, an emphasis that can provide the stimulus for creative dialogue and shared action between Jews, Muslims, and Christians with regard to the responsible stewardship and management of the world's resources, though there may never be more than an agreement to differ as far as theological issues are concerned.

DIVERSITY

The Jewish world reflects the pluralistic nature of the wider society in which Jews live. All Jews today contend with conflicting influences. One option is to cut off modern influences as far as possible, and seek refuge in tradition. Another is to abandon Judaism. The path that young Jews are increasingly choosing goes beyond the fractiousness between and within different groups with regard to authority, Torah, the role of women, modernity and cultural change and the state of Israel, and seeks to transform Judaism. But it is a mistake to define movements within modern Judaism as if they were sects or denominations. It is more accurate to use the term 'schools of thought'. There is a saying among Jews, 'Where you have two Jews you will have three opinions.'

THE FUTURE

The continuity of Judaism cannot be taken for granted. People are freer to be Jews than at any other time in history. They are also freer not to be. There is real concern about the continuation of the Jewish faith when in the United States one in two Jews either does not marry or marries a non-Jew. The long and painful history of anti-Semitism has understandably made some people uncertain about wanting their children to be overtly Jewish. There are many examples of people changing their name in order to hide their Jewishness.

JEWISH POPULATION FIGURES BY CONTINENT IN 2004

	Jewish Population
Africa	87,900
Asia	5,047,300
Europe	1,577,000
North America	6,114,500
South America	365,500
Oceania	103,000
Total	13,295,200

A new generation of Jews sometimes express a desire to be free of the burden of memory that has traditionally been the hallmark of being Jewish. In complex, pluralist, and multicultural societies, some argue that Jewish identity has become superfluous. However, Jews and Judaism have an incredible capacity to survive.

There is also today a greater confidence in the continuation of the story that is Judaism than there has been since the Holocaust. Jewish people have managed to outlive a succession of oppressors. At the same time, they have increased the depth and richness of Jewish spirituality. More non-Jews than ever before find inspiration from the study of Judaism, as it has entered the curriculum of institutions of higher learning.

With rising levels of anti-Semitism across the world, the need for education and dialogue is acute. Contrary to many people's perceptions, Judaism combines universalism with the exclusivity of an ethnic religion. Jewish ideas of salvation extend to the non-Jewish world. Neither Christianity nor Islam would be conceivable without Judaism. Since the Holocaust, many Christians have commenced a more positive exploration of their Jewish roots. The monotheistic religions share a distinctive ethical focus that can inspire greater efforts on the part of human beings to work together to perfect the world.

LIZ RAMSEY

QUESTIONS

1. Explain the differences between the religion of the ancient Judeans and rabbinic Judaism.

2. What were the implications for Judaism of the destruction of the Temple in 70 CE?

3. Why was medieval Europe often such an inhospitable place for Jews?

4. Explain the importance of the covenant to Judaism.

5. How important are Maimonides' Thirteen Principles of the Faith for Judaism?

6. Explain the different roles of *Tanakh*, Mishnah, and Talmud in rabbinic Judaism.

7. Why are there such different views within Judaism about the coming of the Messiah?

8. Explain the main differences between Orthodox and Reform Judaism.

9. Why is the state of Israel so important in Judaism today?

10. How is modern Judaism able to contain such diverse views on questions of belief and practice?

FURTHER READING

Barnavi, Elie, ed., *A Historical Atlas of the Jewish People: From the Time of the Patriarchs to the Present*. New York: Knopf, 1992.

Biale, David, ed., *Cultures of the Jews: A New History*. New York: Schocken Books, 2002.

Cesarani, David, *Final Solution: The Fate of the Jews 1933–1949*. Macmillan, 2016.

Friedman, Richard E., *The Bible with Sources Revealed*. San Francisco: Harper, 2003.

Gaster, Theodor H., *The Festivals of the Jewish Year*. New York: William Sloane Associates, 1952.

Newman, Louis I., ed., *The Hasidic Anthology: Tales and Teachings of the Hasidim*. New York: Scribner, 1934.

Schama, Simon, *The Story of the Jews and the Fate of the World*. London: Bodley Head, 2013.

Seltzer, Tobert, *Jewish People, Jewish Thought*. New York: Macmillan 1980.

Steinsaltz, Adin, *The Talmud, the Steinsaltz Edition: A Reference Guide*. New York: Random House, 1989.

Steinsaltz, Adin, *A Guide to Jewish Prayer*. New York: Schocken, 2002.

GALLERY

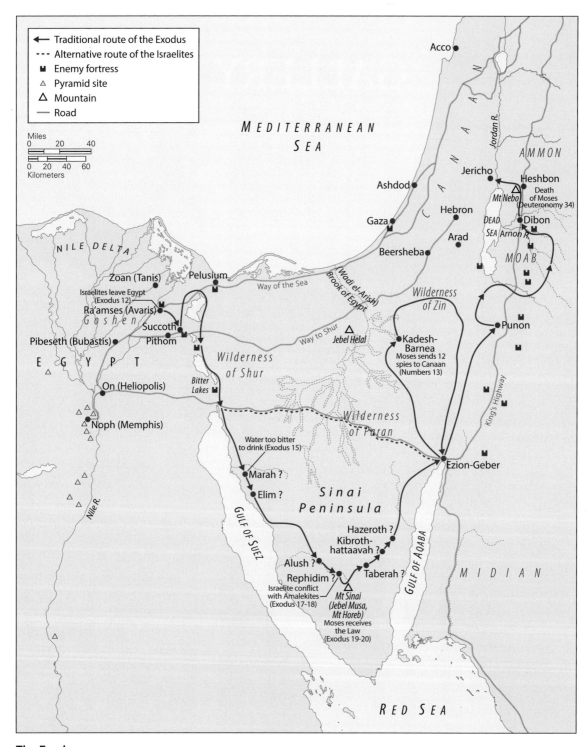

The Exodus

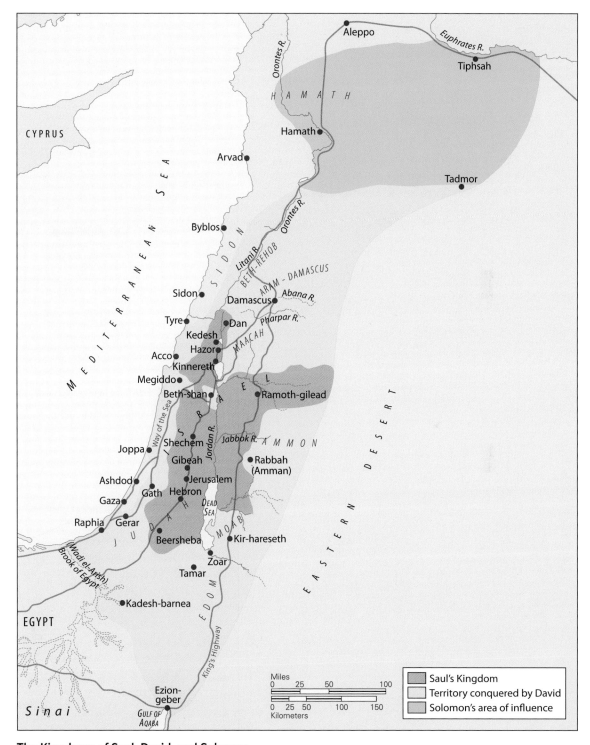

The Kingdoms of Saul, David, and Solomon

Map labels:

CYPRUS

MEDITERRANEAN SEA

Aleppo
Tiphsah
Euphrates R.
Orontes R.
HAMATH
Hamath
Tadmor
Arvad
Byblos
SIDON
Litani R.
BETH-REHOB
Orontes R.
ARAM – DAMASCUS
Sidon
Damascus
Abana R.
Tyre
Dan
Pharpar R.
Kedesh
MAACAH
Acco
Hazor
Kinnereth
Megiddo
Beth-shan
Ramoth-gilead
I S R A E L
Way of the Sea
Jordan R.
Jabbok R.
AMMON
Joppa
Shechem
Gibeah
Rabbah
(Amman)
Ashdod
Jerusalem
Gath
Hebron
Gaza
DEAD SEA
Raphia
Gerar
Beersheba
Kir-haresheth
J U D A H
MOAB
Zoar
Tamar
EDOM
(Wadi el-Arish)
Brook of Egypt
Kadesh-barnea
EGYPT
King's Highway
EASTERN DESERT
Ezion-geber
Sinai
GULF OF AQABA

Scale:

Miles
0   25   50   100

0   25   50   100   150
Kilometers

Legend:

- Saul's Kingdom
- Territory conquered by David
- Solomon's area of influence

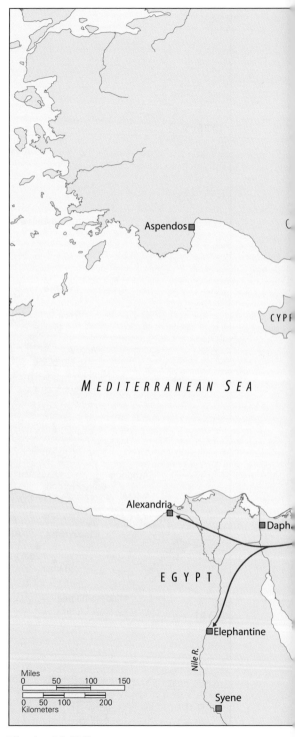

The Jewish Exiles

A BRIEF INTRODUCTION TO JUDAISM

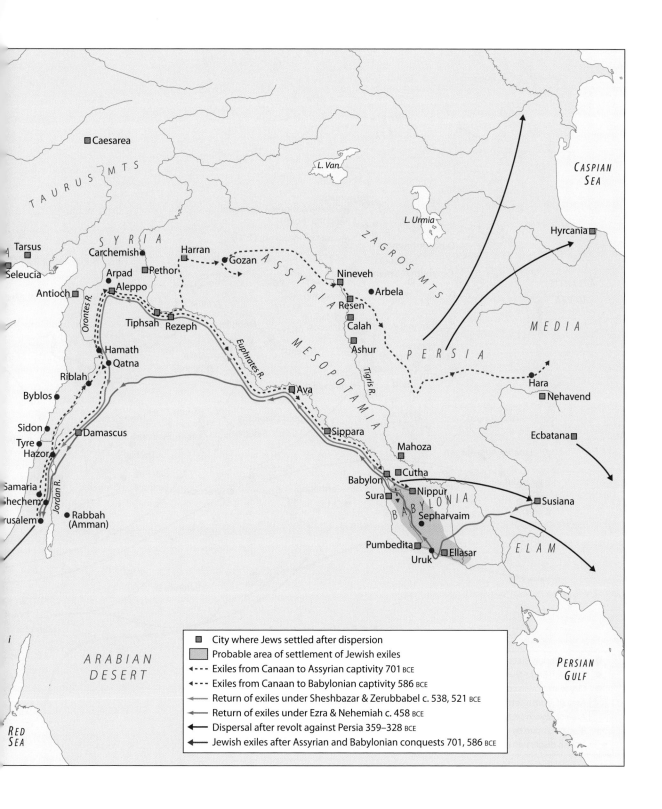

Caesarea

TAURUS MTS

L. Van

CASPIAN SEA

L. Urmia

Hyrcania

Tarsus
Seleucia

SYRIA

Carchemish
Harran
Gozan

ZAGROS MTS

Nineveh

MEDIA

Arpad Pethor
Antioch
Aleppo

ASSYRIA

Arbela
Resen
Calah

Orontes R.

Tiphsah Rezeph

Ashur

PERSIA

Hamath
Qatna

Euphrates R.

MESOPOTAMIA

Tigris R.

Hara
Nehavend

Riblah

Ava

Ecbatana

Byblos

Sidon
Tyre
Hazor

Damascus

Sippara

Mahoza

Cutha

Susiana

Babylon
Sura Nippur

Jordan R.

Samaria
Shechem
Jerusalem

Rabbah
(Amman)

BABYLONIA

Sepharvaim

ELAM

Pumbedita
Uruk

Ellasar

PERSIAN GULF

ARABIAN DESERT

RED SEA

■ City where Jews settled after dispersion

▨ Probable area of settlement of Jewish exiles

◄--- Exiles from Canaan to Assyrian captivity 701 BCE

◄--- Exiles from Canaan to Babylonian captivity 586 BCE

◄— Return of exiles under Sheshbazar & Zerubbabel c. 538, 521 BCE

◄— Return of exiles under Ezra & Nehemiah c. 458 BCE

◄— Dispersal after revolt against Persia 359–328 BCE

◄— Jewish exiles after Assyrian and Babylonian conquests 701, 586 BCE

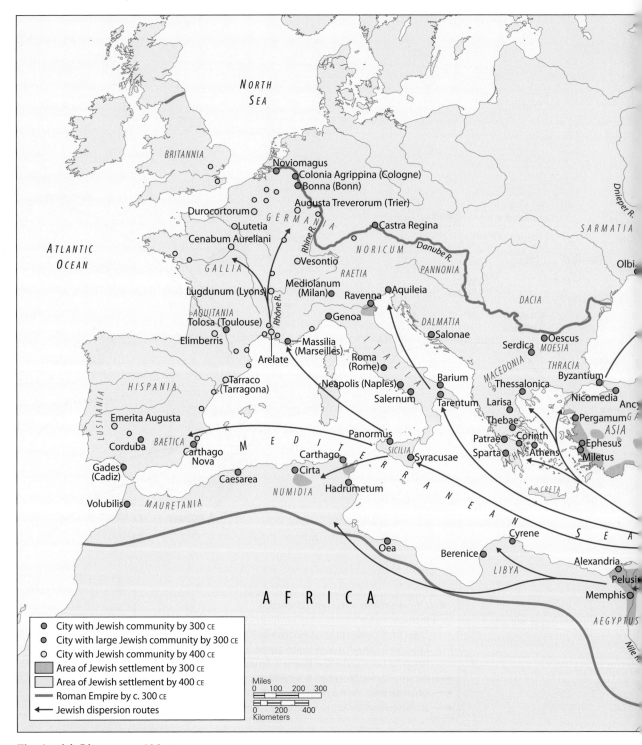

The Jewish Diaspora c. 400 CE

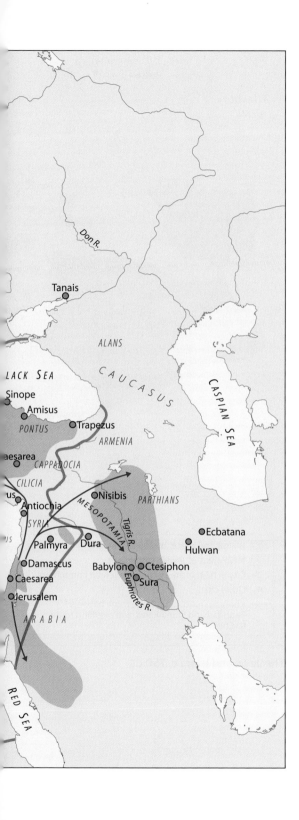

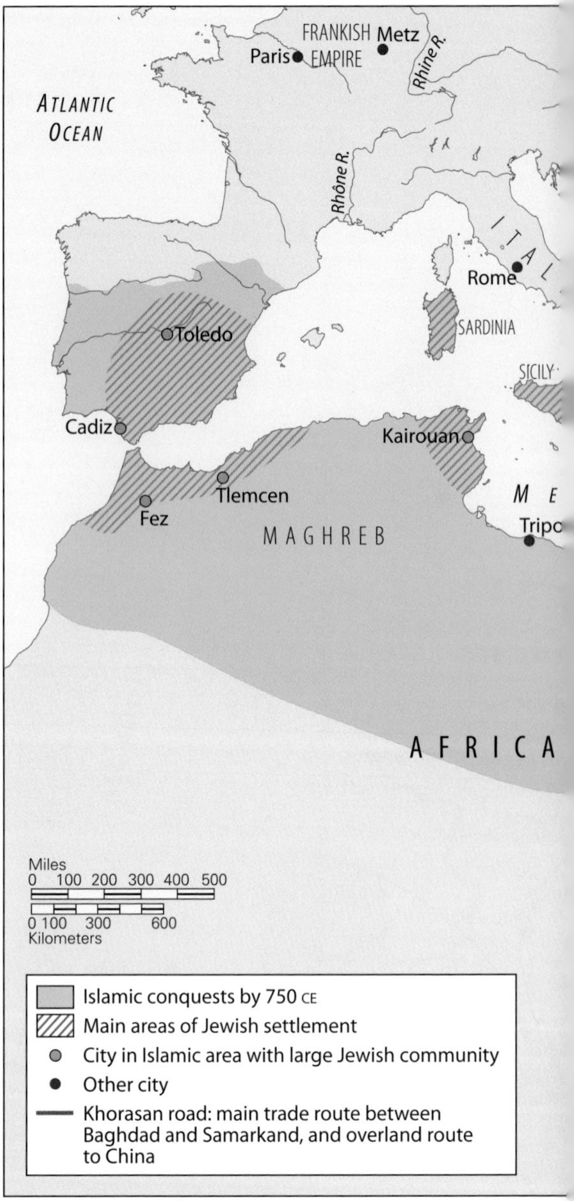
FRANKISH EMPIRE
Metz
Paris
Rhine R.
ATLANTIC OCEAN
Rhône R.
ITAL
Rome
Toledo
SARDINIA
SICILY
Cadiz
Kairouan
Tlemcen
Fez
ME
Tripo
MAGHREB
AFRICA
Miles
0 100 200 300 400 500
0 100 300 600
Kilometers
Islamic conquests by 750 CE
Main areas of Jewish settlement
City in Islamic area with large Jewish community
Other city
Khorasan road: main trade route between Baghdad and Samarkand, and overland route to China

The Jews and Islam c. 750 CE

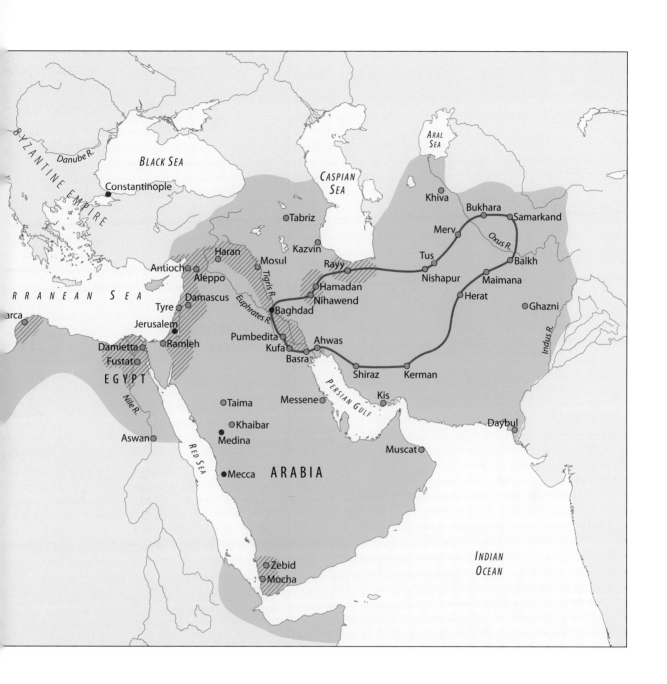

Judaism in 16th and 17th Century Europe

Western Ashenazi Jews
Eastern Ashkenazi Jews
Sephardic Jews
Italian Jews (=Roman)
← Major Jewish migration
◇ Yeshivah (Rabbinic school)
▲ Karaite centre
■ Kabbalist or Sabbataean centre

A BRIEF INTRODUCTION TO JUDAISM

BALTIC SEA

RUSSIA

Birzai

Vilna
Königsberg
Grodno   Trakal   Minsk
PRUSSIA   Sluck
POLAND
Poznan   Brest-Litovsk   Pinsk
Berlin   Warsaw
Amsterdam   Lublin
Cologne   Dresden   Ludmir   Kiev
NETHERLANDS   Breslau   Lvov   Ostrog
Frankfurt   Prague   Luck   Derazne
Rhine R.   Krakov   Halicz   Dnieper R.
Nickelsburg   Don R.
Strasburg   Augsburg   Danube R.
Munich   Vienna
AUSTRIA   Budapest
Pavia   Padua   HUNGARY
Cremona   Mantua   Venice
Rhône R.   Belgrade   Bucharest
Livorno   BLACK SEA
ITALY   Ulcini   Sofia
Rome   Edirne   Constantinople
OTTOMAN   EMPIRE
Naples   Salonica
Smyrna (Izmir)
MEDITERRANEAN   SEA
Euphrates R.
Safed
Jerusalem
AFRICA   Cairo
EGYPT
Nile R.   RED SEA

Miles
100 200 300 400 500
100 300 500 700
Kilometers

Interior of the Old Portuguese Synagogue, Amsterdam, known as the Esnoga or Snoge, opened in 1675.

A BRIEF INTRODUCTION TO JUDAISM

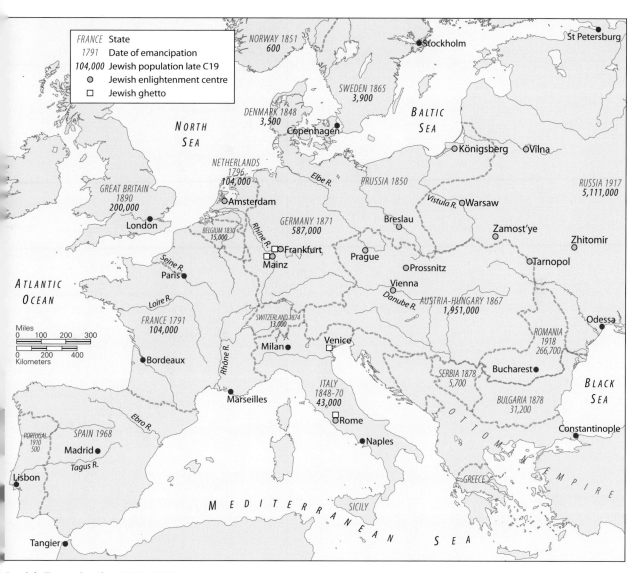

NORWAY 1851
600

NORTH SEA

SWEDEN 1865
3,900

●Stockholm

St Petersburg

BALTIC SEA

DENMARK 1848
3,500

Copenhagen

●Königsberg   ○Vilna

NETHERLANDS
1796
104,000

GREAT BRITAIN
1890
200,000

PRUSSIA 1850

RUSSIA 1917
5,111,000

Elbe R.

Vistula R. ○Warsaw

London

○Amsterdam

BELGIUM 1830
15,000

GERMANY 1871
587,000

Breslau●

Zamost'ye

Zhitomir
○

Rhine R.

□○Frankfurt
□□
Mainz

○Prague

○Prossnitz

Tarnopol
○

Seine R.

Paris●

ATLANTIC OCEAN

Loire R.

FRANCE 1791
104,000

SWITZERLAND 1874
13,000

Vienna
○

Danube R.

AUSTRIA-HUNGARY 1867
1,951,000

Odessa
○

Miles
0 100 200 300
0   200   400
Kilometers

Rhône R.

Milan●

Venice
□

ROMANIA
1918
266,700

Bordeaux●

Marseilles●

ITALY
1848-70
43,000

SERBIA 1878
5,700

Bucharest●

BLACK SEA

Ebro R.

□Rome

BULGARIA 1878
31,200

Constantinople

PORTUGAL
1910
500

SPAIN 1968
500

Madrid●

Tagus R.

Naples

OTTOMAN EMPIRE

Lisbon

GREECE

Tangier●

M E D I T E R R A N E A N   S E A

SICILY

Jewish Emancipation 1789–1918

The Origins of Judaism in the USA

A BRIEF INTRODUCTION TO JUDAISM

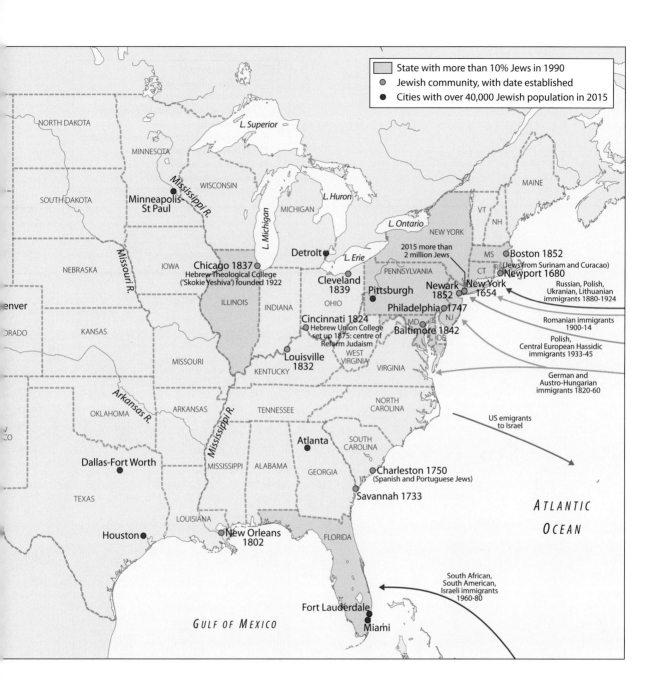

NORTH DAKOTA

MINNESOTA

L. Superior

WISCONSIN

L. Huron

MICHIGAN

L. Michigan

L. Ontario

NEW YORK

MAINE

VT

NH

SOUTH DAKOTA

Minneapolis-St Paul

Mississippi R.

NEBRASKA

Missouri R.

IOWA

Chicago 1837
Hebrew Theological College
('Skokie Yeshiva') founded 1922

Detroit

L. Erie

Cleveland
1839

Pittsburgh

2015 more than
2 million Jews

Newark New York
1852   1654

Boston 1852

Newport 1680
(Jews from Surinam and Curacao)

Russian, Polish,
Ukranian, Lithuanian
immigrants 1880-1924

MS

CT

RI

enver

ORADO

CO

KANSAS

MISSOURI

INDIANA

ILLINOIS

OHIO

PENNSYLVANIA

Philadelphia 1747

NJ

Romanian immigrants
1900-14

Cincinnati 1824
Hebrew Union College
set up 1875: centre of
Reform Judaism

Baltimore 1842

MD

DE

Polish,
Central European Hassidic
immigrants 1933-45

Louisville
1832

WEST
VIRGINIA

KENTUCKY

VIRGINIA

German and
Austro-Hungarian
immigrants 1820-60

OKLAHOMA

ARKANSAS

TENNESSEE

Arkansas R.

Mississippi R.

NORTH
CAROLINA

US emigrants
to Israel

Atlanta

SOUTH
CAROLINA

Dallas-Fort Worth

MISSISSIPPI

ALABAMA

GEORGIA

Charleston 1750
(Spanish and Portuguese Jews)

TEXAS

LOUISIANA

Savannah 1733

ATLANTIC
OCEAN

Houston

New Orleans
1802

FLORIDA

South African,
South American,
Israeli immigrants
1960-80

Fort Lauderdale

GULF OF MEXICO

Miami

Legend:
☐ State with more than 10% Jews in 1990
● Jewish community, with date established
● Cities with over 40,000 Jewish population in 2015

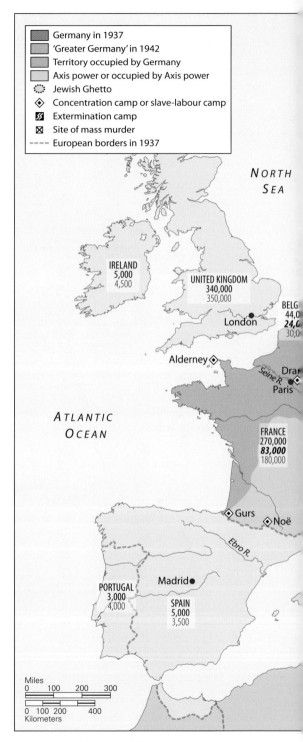

NORTH
SEA

IRELAND
5,000
4,500

UNITED KINGDOM
340,000
350,000

BELG
44,0
24,0
30,0

London

Alderney◇

Dra
Paris◇
Seine R.

ATLANTIC
OCEAN

FRANCE
270,000
83,000
180,000

◇Gurs   ◇Noë

Ebro R.

Madrid●

PORTUGAL
3,000
4,000

SPAIN
5,000
3,500

Miles
0   100   200   300

0   100 200   400
Kilometers

Judaism and the Third Reich

FINLAND
2,000
1,800

NORWAY
2,000
870
1,000

SWEDEN
10,000
22,000

Klooga

ESTONIA
5,000
1,000
500

Vaivara

R U S S I A

LATVIA
94,000
80,000
12,000

Riga
Kaiserwald

*BALTIC
SEA*

LITHUANIA
160,000
135,000
20,000

Kaunas

Vilna

Moscow

DENMARK
7,000
120
5,500

ERLANDS
5,000
6,000
,000

Stutthof

Ponary

Minsk
Trostenets

Neuengamme

Ravensbrück

POLAND
3,275,000
4,565,000
(with Lithuania)
120,000

Bialystok

Treblinka

Bergen-Belsen

Sachsenhausen

Berlin

Westerbork

Niederhagen

Chelm

Warsaw

ogenbusch

Mittelbau-
Dora

Bernburg

Gross Rosen

Lodz

Sobibor

Kiev

erdam

Buchenwald

Lublin

Majdanek

GERMANY
365,000
125,000
85,000

Theresienstadt

Czestochawa
Sosnoviec

Krakow-
Plaszow

Belzek

Brody

LUX.
3,000
700
500

Prague

Auschwitz

Strysnow

Lvov

Babi-Yar

Flossenberg

Brno

Natzweiler-
Struthof

Mauthausen

Nitra

CZECHOSLOVAKIA
360,000 – *277,000*
55,000

Bar

Balanowka

Dachau

Danube R.

Edineti

Bogdanowka

AUSTRIA
180,000 – *70,000*
16,000

Budapest

HUNGARY
440,000 – *300,000*
200,000

Odessa

SWITZERLAND
20,000
35,000

ROMANIA
800,000
264,000
300,000

Jasenovac

ITALY
50,000
7,500
52,000

Gospic

Zemun

Sajmiste

ADRIATIC SEA

YUGOSLAVIA
75,000
60,000
10,500

Sofia

BULGARIA
50,000
46,500

BLACK SEA

Les Milles

Rome

GREECE
75,000
65,000
10,500

TURKEY
75,000
80,000

MEDITERRANEAN

SEA

Rhine R.

nelen

Legend box:

GERMANY — Country
365,000 — Jews pre-war
125,000 — Approx number of Jews killed
85,000 — Numbers of Jews post war

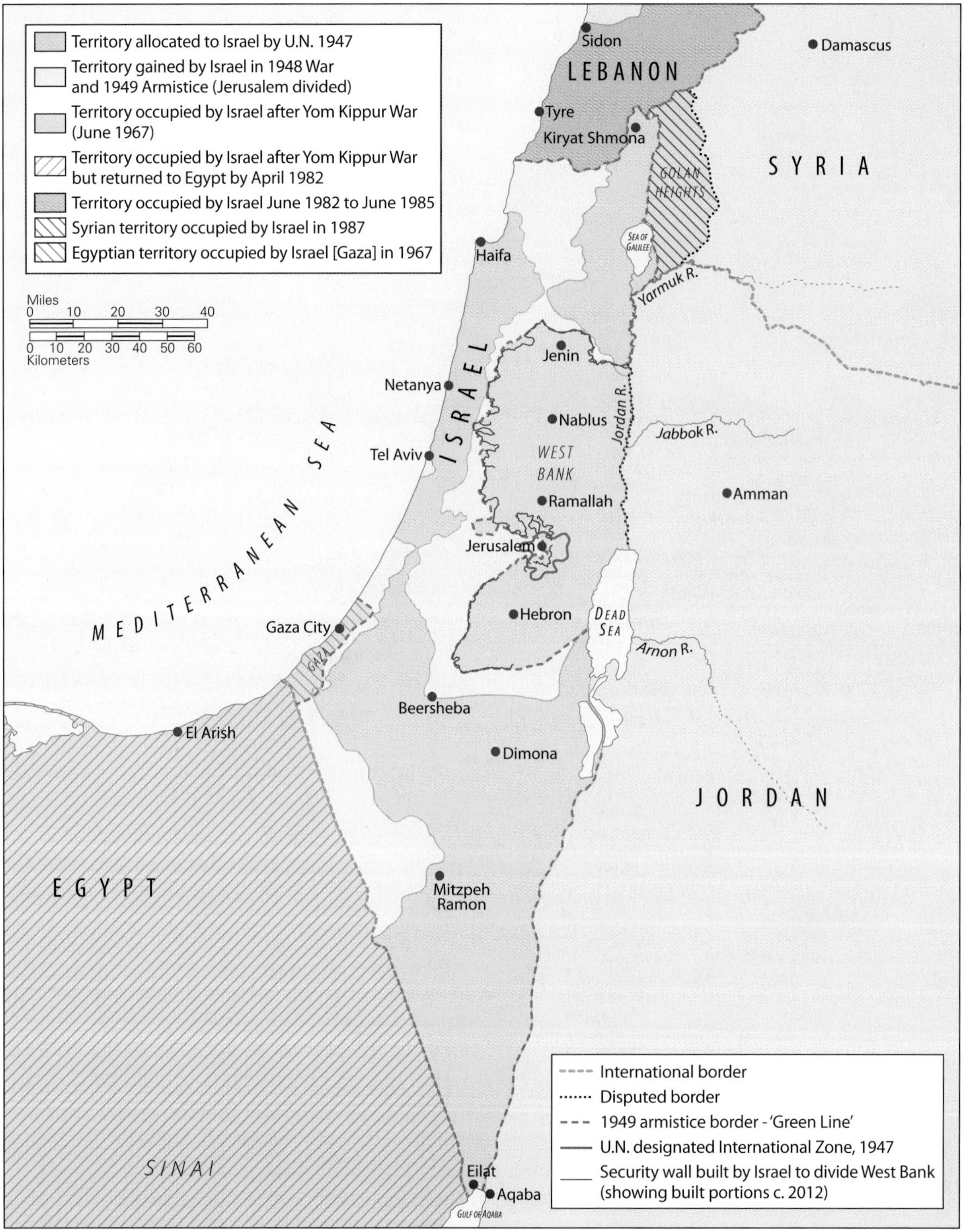
Territory allocated to Israel by U.N. 1947
Territory gained by Israel in 1948 War and 1949 Armistice (Jerusalem divided)
Territory occupied by Israel after Yom Kippur War (June 1967)
Territory occupied by Israel after Yom Kippur War but returned to Egypt by April 1982
Territory occupied by Israel June 1982 to June 1985
Syrian territory occupied by Israel in 1987
Egyptian territory occupied by Israel [Gaza] in 1967
Miles
0 10 20 30 40
0 10 20 30 40 50 60
Kilometers
Sidon
Damascus
LEBANON
Tyre
Kiryat Shmona
SYRIA
GOLAN HEIGHTS
Haifa
SEA OF GALILEE
Yarmuk R.
Jenin
Netanya
ISRAEL
Nablus
Jordan R.
Jabbok R.
MEDITERRANEAN SEA
Tel Aviv
WEST BANK
Ramallah
Amman
Jerusalem
Hebron
DEAD SEA
Gaza City
GAZA
Arnon R.
Beersheba
El Arish
Dimona
JORDAN
EGYPT
Mitzpeh Ramon
SINAI
Eilat
Aqaba
GULF OF AQABA
International border
Disputed border
1949 armistice border - 'Green Line'
U.N. designated International Zone, 1947
Security wall built by Israel to divide West Bank (showing built portions c. 2012)

The Modern State of Israel

Rapid Fact-Finder

A

Abraham, Isaac, and Jacob The three patriarchs who are continually remembered in the Jewish liturgy as the original recipients of God's promise and blessing. According to tradition they are buried in the tomb of the patriarchs in the cave of Machpelah in the modern town of Hebron.

Absolute, The Term for God or the divine often preferred by those who conceive of God predominantly in abstract or impersonal terms.

Adonai *see* Yhwh.

Afterlife Any form of conscious existence after the death of the body.

Agadah/Aggadah A moral or devotional Jewish teaching derived from the midrashic exposition of a Hebrew text (*see* Midrash). There are many of them in the Talmud where they take the form of narrative tales, poems, and metaphysical speculations.

Akiva, Rabbi (c. 50–135 CE) Jewish teacher who developed the Mishnah method of repetitive transmission of teachings. He began the work of systematizing the available interpretations of the Torah, laying the foundations for the work of Judah HaNasi. He was also famous for his use of midrash, investing every detail of the Hebrew texts with significance.

Amidah ('standing') The principal Jewish daily prayer, also known as the Eighteen Benedictions, recited standing. Today it actually comprises nineteen benedictions, including prayers for the restoration of Israel and for peace.

Ancestor veneration The practice in indigenous religions of making offerings to the spirits of the dead and expecting to communicate with them through dreams.

Angels Spiritual beings who in Judaism and Christianity act as the messengers of God. They have two primary functions: to worship God, and to support and encourage human beings. In Islam the Archangel Gabriel (Jibril) is associated with the giving of the Qur'an.

Animism A term formerly used to describe pre-literary religions. It was dropped because its meaning, 'spiritism', was felt to be misleading.

Apocalyptic Genre of writing in Christianity and Judaism, concerned with hidden truths, pointing to the ultimate triumph of faith and the judgment of nations. Daniel and Revelation are examples in the Bible.

Apocrypha Historical and wisdom writings found in the Greek version of the Hebrew scriptures but excluded from the canon of the Hebrew Bible. The Roman Catholic Church and Eastern Orthodox churches accept its authority, but Protestant churches distinguish it from inspired scripture.

Ark (1) Israelite religious artefact, probably in the form of a portable miniature temple, which was carried into battle as evidence of the presence of God (*see* Yhwh). In Solomon's Temple the ark lived in the Holy of Holies. (2) A cupboard in the wall of a synagogue that faces Jerusalem, where the handwritten parchment scrolls of the Torah are kept.

Asceticism Austere practices designed to lead to the control of the body and the senses. These may include fasting and meditation, the renunciation of possessions, and the pursuit of solitude.

Ashkenazim One of the two main cultural groups in Judaism which emerged in the Middle Ages. Their tradition is from Palestinian Jewry and they live in Central, Northern, and Eastern Europe. They developed Yiddish as their language, which is a mixture of Hebrew, Slav, and German. *See also* Sephardim.

Atonement Ritual act which restores harmony between the human and the divine when it has been broken by sin or impurity

Atonement, Day of *see* Yom Kippur.

Austerity Ascetic practice in which one exercises self-restraint or denial, for example, the restriction of food during a fast.

Ayn Sof *see* Ein Sof.

B

Baal Divinity of ancient Canaanite or Phoenician fertility religion. The name means 'lord'.

Baal Shem Tov (1698–1760 CE) Jewish mystic who founded the movement of Hasidism. His name means 'Master of the Good Name' and it is often shortened to the Besht. His original name was Israel ben Eliezer. At the age of thirty-six he developed powers of healing and prophecy. He taught a kind of mystical pantheism. He was greatly loved and became the source of many Yiddish legends and miracle stories.

Babylonian flood story A parallel to the story of the flood in the Bible going back to a Sumerian original but best known from the Epic of Gilgamesh. It tells the story of a wise king, Ut-napishtim, who survived the flood caused by the god Enlil by taking refuge in a huge boat with his wife and various animals. He was rewarded by Enlil by being transported to a land of immortality.

Bar Mitzvah ('Son of the Commandment') Ceremony by which Jewish boys, at the age of thirteen, accept the positive commandments of Judaism and are counted as adult members of the community.

Bat Mitzvah ('Daughter of the Commandment') Ceremony, mainly in non-Orthodox communities, by which Jewish girls, at the age of twelve, accept the positive commandments of Judaism and are counted as adult members of the community.

Bible The book of Christianity, comprising the Hebrew Old Testament and the New Testament which, Christians believe, together form a unified message of God's salvation.

Booths/Tabernacles/Sukkot Jewish festival marking the end of the harvest. Branch- or straw-covered booths remind Jews of God's protection during their forty-year journey through the wilderness.

Buber, Martin (1878–1965 CE) Austrian–Jewish theologian whose religious roots were in Hasidism. Although a Zionist, he was critical of the politics of Zionism and of

Talmudic tradition (*see* Talmud). He believed that the central task of Jews was to build up God's kingdom on the basis of the Jewish belief in an essential dialogue between God and humanity. He has influenced Christian spirituality and social teaching.

C

Chant Type of singing in which many syllables are sung on a single note or a repeated short musical phrase. Many religions use chanting in worship. Jews and Christians chant the psalms; Buddhists and others their own sacred scriptures. The repetitive nature of chanting can aid meditation.

Circumcision The cutting off of the prepuce in males or the internal labia in females as a religious rite. It is widely practised in traditional African religion, either shortly after birth or at puberty. In Judaism boys are circumcised at eight days of age in commemoration of Abraham's covenant with God. Male converts to Judaism undergo this rite.

Civil religion Religion as a system of beliefs, symbols, and practices which legitimate the authority of a society's institutions and bind people together in the public sphere.

Conservative Judaism Movement which tries to stand midway between Orthodox and Progressive Judaism. It claims to accept the Talmudic tradition (*see* Talmud) but to interpret the Torah in the light of modern needs.

Conversion A moral or spiritual change of direction, or the adoption of religious beliefs not previously held.

Covenant A bargain or agreement. In Judaism the chief reference is to that made with Moses at Sinai: God, having liberated his people from Egypt, promises them the land of Israel and his blessing and protection as long as they keep the Torah. This confirms the earlier covenants with Abraham and with Noah. The term is also used of God's special relationship with the house of David. With the defeat of the Kingdom of Judah in 586 BCE, Jeremiah's prophecy of a new covenant written on the people's hearts came into its own.

Creation The act of God by which the universe came into being. Hence also refers to the universe itself. In Judaism, Christianity, and Islam creation is usually thought of as being *ex nihilo*, from out of nothing that existed before.

D

David King of the Israelite tribes around 1000–962 BCE who united them and extended their territory. He stormed the city of the Jebusites and made it his capital, Jerusalem. He was a musician and poet, to whom a number of psalms in the Bible are ascribed. The belief is common to Judaism and Christianity that the Messiah would be a descendant of David.

Dead Sea Scrolls Sacred writings of a breakaway Jewish sect which were discovered in 1947 at Qumran on the western shore of the Dead Sea. The several scrolls and fragments include much of the Hebrew Bible as well as hymns, treatises, and rules for the life of the sect. Many scholars identify the sect with the Essenes.

Demonology Teaching about the demonic and all forms of personified evil.

Devil Term generally used to describe an evil spirit.

Diaspora (1) The geographical spread of a people who share a common culture. (2) The term was originally used to describe the spread of the Jewish nation, the dispersion from the land of Israel. The dispersion of the Jews came about partly as a result of war and exile, partly as a result of travel and trade.

Dietary laws Rules about food and drink that are characteristic of a particular religion. Thus Judaism prohibits the simultaneous preparation or eating of milk and meat products, bans totally the eating of, for example, pork and shellfish, and regulates the ritual slaughter of other animals for meat.

Disciple Followers of a religious leader or teaching.

Divinities Name given to minor gods or spirits in indigenous religions who rule over an area of the world or some human activity – e.g. storms, war, farming, marriage. Divinities are usually worshipped formally with special rituals and festivals.

Doctrine A religious teaching or belief which is taught and upheld within a particular religious community.

Dreams may contain warnings or commands or promises of blessing.

E

Election God's choice of Israel to be his people as expressed in the covenant at Mount Sinai and manifested in the gift of the land of Israel. In Judaism the election of the Jews carries responsibility. They are to bear witness to the reality of God in the world by keeping the Torah. In Christian theology, the concept is widened to include Gentile converts to Christianity who spiritually inherit the promises made to the Patriarchs and to Moses.

Eliezer, Israel ben *see* Baal Shem Tov.

Elohim Plural form of the Canaanite word for a divinity (*see* divinities), usually translated 'God' and used as a name of God by the Hebrews (*see also* El). It is sometimes treated as a common-noun plural, 'gods' or 'angels'. (*See also* angels.)

Ein Sof Name for God used in Jewish mysticism, in particular in the Kabbalah, meaning the endless, the absolute infinite whose essence is unrevealed and unknowable.

Esoteric Word meaning 'inner', suggesting something (e.g. a knowledge or a teaching) that is available only for the specially initiated and secret from outsiders and perhaps even from ordinary believers.

Essenes Jewish group which withdrew to live a monastic life in the Dead Sea area during the Roman period. Most were celibate and they stressed the importance of asceticism. They also performed exorcisms and rites of spiritual healing. Many scholars believe that the Dead Sea Scrolls were the scriptures of an Essene community.

Exile (1) The period between 597 BCE and around 538 BCE when leading Jews from the former Jewish kingdoms were held in captivity in Babylon. (2) The condition of Jewish life in the diaspora, away from the land of Israel.

Exodus The flight of the people of Israel from Egypt under the leadership of Moses.

A BRIEF INTRODUCTION TO JUDAISM

Exorcism Removal of sin or evil, particularly an evil spirit in possession of someone, by prayer or ritual action.

Ezra Scribe of the Babylonian exile who was sent with a royal warrant from the Persian king to reform religion in Jerusalem. Traditionally he arrived in 458 BCE and embarked on a programme to purify the Jewish faith and install the Torah as the central authority in Jewish life.

F

Faith Attitude of belief, in trust and commitment to a divine being or a religious teaching. It can also refer to the beliefs of a religion, 'the faith', which is passed on from teachers to believers.

Fall of Jerusalem The capture of Jerusalem and the final destruction of the Temple of Jerusalem by the Roman general Titus in 70 CE at the end of a revolt which broke out in 66 CE.

Fasting Total or partial abstinence from food, undertaken as a religious discipline. In indigenous religions it is often a preparation for a ceremony of initiation. In Judaism and Christianity it is a sign of mourning or repentance for sin. It is also more generally used as a means of gaining clarity of vision and mystical insight.

G

Gabriel An archangel named in both the Old and New Testaments. In the Gospel of Luke he foretells the births of John the Baptist and Jesus.

Gemara Part of the Jewish Talmud that takes the form of a series of rabbinical commentaries on the Mishnah.

Gentile Person who is not a Jew.

God (1) The creator and sustainer of the universe; the absolute being on whom all that is depends. (2) A being with divine power and attributes; a deity, a major Divinity.

Goddess (1) Female form of god. (2) The supreme being conceived as female as in some modern Pagan religious movements. Worshippers of the Goddess claim that they are continuing the ancient religion of the Mother Goddess who was a personification of nature.

H

Hades Greek name for the underworld, the abode of the dead. In the Septuagint version of the Hebrew Bible it translates *sheol*. In Christian usage it is sometimes used for the interim abode of the departed as distinguished from Hell, the abode of the damned.

Hagadah/Haggadah Prayer-book used by Jews on the eve of Passover for the Seder ritual.

Halakhah (from Hebrew verb 'to walk') A legal teaching based on the midrashic exposition of a Hebrew text (*see* Midrash).

Hamartiology Teaching about sin.

Hanukkah ('dedication') Eight-day Jewish festival marked by the lighting of ritual candles which celebrates the rededication of the Temple of Jerusalem by Judas Maccabeus in 164 BCE.

Hasidim ('the pious') Followers of Baal Shem Tov, who taught a new kind of Hasidism in the eighteenth century CE.

Hasidism Jewish mystical movement with roots in the Kabbalah which arose in the eighteenth century in response to the teachings of Baal Shem Tov after a period of persecution by the Cossacks. It stressed the presence of God in everyday life and the value of prayer. Chanting and dancing were used as aids to ecstatic communion with God. The movement was popular and had a wide appeal among ordinary Jews.

Heaven (1) The realm of God or of the gods. (2) In Christianity the dwelling place of God and the ultimate home of the saved, regarded both as a place and a state.

Hebrew (1) A member of the Semitic tribes which emerged as the people of Israel. (2) The (Semitic) language of the ancient people of Israel, of the Hebrew Bible, and of the modern state of Israel.

Hebrew Bible The Jewish scriptures which comprise the Books of the Law (*see* Torah), the Prophets, and the Writings. According to tradition, the canon was fixed at the Synod of Jamnia or Yavne about 100 CE.

Hell Realm where the wicked go after death. Religious teachings differ over whether this punishment is reformatory or eternal. In Christianity, it is total separation from God. Most religions describe a place or a condition for the wicked following death. Zoroastrianism, Judaism, and Islam all describe such a state following divine judgment after death.

Hellenism The adoption of the Greek language, culture, philosophy, and ideas, particularly around the Mediterranean, from the time of Alexander the Great (356–323 BCE). It was the dominant cultural influence during the rise of Christianity.

Herzl, Theodor (1860–1904 CE) Leader of the Zionist movement (*see* Zionism). He argued that a national homeland for the Jews was a necessity. He travelled widely raising support from Christian governments for the Zionist cause and convened the First Zionist Congress in 1897 which formulated a political programme for the return to Palestine.

High Priest Traditional head of the Jewish priesthood and organizer of temple worship. His function was to enter the Holy of Holies and offer sacrifice on the Day of Atonement. This was a key political appointment under the Seleucids and Romans. Talmudic tradition criticizes the corruption of some who held the office, which ceased at the destruction of the Temple in 70 CE.

Hillel Pharisaic Jewish teacher of the first century CE. He was known for his humane and lenient interpretations of the Torah, in contrast to his chief opponent, the stern and religious Shammai.

Holiness The sacred power, strangeness, and otherness of the divine. In the Bible and the Qur'an the term has moral implications and refers to God's purity and righteousness as well as to that which invokes awe.

Holocaust (from the Latin Bible's word for 'whole burnt offering') The name given to Hitler's extermination of six million Jews in the Nazi death camps in Europe from 1941–45. Mass destruction was envisaged as the 'final solution' to the 'problem' of the Jews. The memory of the Holocaust is the key to modern Jewish theology and made the founding of the state of Israel an event of profound significance. The Holocaust is also referred to by many Jews as as the *Shoah* (catastrophe).

Holy Spirit The third person of the Christian Trinity. In the Bible the Holy Spirit is the instrument of divine action and is portrayed as fire or wind. In this sense the Spirit is acknowledged in Judaism and Islam.

Humanism Way of life based on the belief that what is good for human beings is the highest good.

I

Incense Sweet-smelling smoke used in worship, made by burning certain aromatic substances.

Inclusive language A response to feminism which tries to eradicate the assumption in speech and writing that maleness is more normally human than femaleness. Churches adopting it modify their hymn, liturgy, and Bible translations.

Independence, Day of Jewish festival of thanksgiving on the anniversary of the birth of the state of Israel (4). The liturgy includes prayers for the victims of the Holocaust.

Indigenous religions The preferred term for religions which are sometimes referred to as 'primal', 'tribal', 'traditional', 'primitive', and 'non-/pre-literate' religions. That said, indigenous religions are often developments of the traditional religions of tribal and aboriginal cultures. The problem with the earlier terminology was that it suggested simple, undeveloped, non-progressive, and archaic belief systems.

Initiation Ceremony marking coming of age, or entry into adult membership of a community. It is also used of the secret ceremonies surrounding membership of the mystery religions.

Intercession Prayer offered on behalf of others by a believer on earth or by a saint in Heaven.

Israel (1) Name given by God to Jacob the patriarch and hence to his descendants, the 'people of Israel'.
(2) The land promised by God to Abram (Abraham) in the early traditions of Judaism.
(3) The Northern Kingdom of Israel which seceded from Solomon's kingdom in 922 BCE and was destroyed by the Assyrians in 722 BCE. (4) The modern state of Israel, founded in Palestine as a Jewish state in 1948 CE.

J

Jehovah *see* Yhwh.

Jerusalem Fortified city captured by David in the c. 1000 BCE which became the capital and principal sanctuary for the people of Israel. It has remained the focus of Jewish religious aspirations and ideals (*see* temple of Jerusalem). It is a holy city for Christians because of its association with the passion, death, and resurrection of Jesus of Nazareth.

Jew (1) A person who is regarded as a member of the Jewish race. According to Jewish religious law Jewishness is inherited through the female line. (2) A person who identifies with Judaism, the religion of the Jews.

Johanan ben Zakkai Creator of the academic Sanhedrin in Jamnia after the Fall of Jerusalem in 70 CE. He led the work of Jewish reconstruction within the limits of Roman law and ensured, through the Sanhedrin, that the Jewish community was represented before the Roman authorities.

Judah HaNasi ('The Prince', 135–217 CE) Leader of the academic Jewish Sanhedrin in Galilee. He was responsible for compiling the Mishnah, which helped the Jewish community in developing a source of ritual authority in religious teaching.

Judaism The religion that developed from the religion of ancient Israel and has been practised ever since by the Jews. It is an ethical monotheism based on the revelation of God to Moses on Mount Sinai and his giving of the Law (*see* Torah). (*See also* Ashkenazim; Conservative Judaism; Orthodox Judaism; Progressive Judaism; Sephardim.)

Judas Maccabeus (d. 160 BCE) Jewish revolutionary who opposed the Hellenizing Seleucid emperor Antiochus Epiphanes, who had set up an image of Olympian Zeus in the Temple of Jerusalem. Under Judas sporadic guerrilla revolt became full-scale war. In 165 BCE Antiochus was defeated and in the following year the temple was rededicated (*see* Hanukkah). Though he achieved religious freedom, he failed to establish a free Jewish state.

Judgment The divine assessment of individuals and the settling of their destinies, a notion found in many religions.

Jung, C. G. (Carl Gustav) (1875–1961 CE) Swiss psychiatrist who invented the theory of archetypes. He investigated the significance of myths, symbols, and dreams, and found in them evidence for a 'collective unconscious' which was at the root of religion.

K

Kabbalah Jewish mystical tradition which flourished in the teaching of two schools: the practical school based in Germany which concentrated in prayer and meditation; the speculative school in Provence and Spain in the thirteenth and fourteenth centuries. The tradition originates in Talmudic speculation on the themes of the work of creation and the divine chariot mentioned in the biblical book of Ezekiel. The most famous Kabbalistic book is *Zohar* ('splendour'), a Midrash on the Pentateuch. (*See* mysticism; Talmud.)

Karaites ('readers of scripture') Heretical Jewish school of the eighth century CE which denied the validity of the Talmud and the oral tradition. They held to a literalist view of the Torah. By the tenth century they had spread throughout the Middle East and Spain. They refused to mix with other Jews. Under attack by Saadya Ben Joseph, the movement gradually disintegrated.

Karo, Joseph (1488–1575 CE) Jewish legal teacher and mystic. He produced the *Shulshan Aruch* (1565), which is one of the most important and cohesive authorities in Judaism, and is considered to be in accord with the purest Talmudic tradition (*see* Talmud). His work is characterized by a devotional tone unusual in legal works.

Kashrut The code in Judaism according to which food is ritually clean or unclean. It refers particularly to meat, which must be slaughtered so as to ensure the minimum of pain and the draining off of blood.

Kingdom of God The rule of God on earth. In Judaism God is king of the universe, the sole creator and ruler. The Jews are his witnesses and their task is to work and pray for the fulfilment of his rule among all people. The kingdom will be brought by the Messiah and will include the restoration of Israel.

Kol Nidrei *see* Yom Kippur.

A BRIEF INTRODUCTION TO JUDAISM

Kook, Abraham Isaac Rabbi (1868–1935 CE) First Chief Rabbi of the Holy Land. He believed the Zionist movement to be essentially religious and that the restoration of Israel was necessary for the redemption of the world. He influenced orthodox Jews in favour of Zionism, though he was also tolerant of secular Jews.

Kotel *see* **Western Wall.**

L

Laity (from Greek laos, 'people') The non-ordained members of a religious community (*see* ordination), or those with no specialist religious function.

Luria, Isaac (CE 1514–72) Jewish teacher from Spain who developed the Kabbalistic teachings of the *Zohar* (*see* Kabbalah). He believed in reincarnation and taught that the dispersion of the Jews was providential and would lead to universal salvation. His teachings inspired devotional poetry and hymns.

M

Maccabees The family and supporters of Judas Maccabeus. They were the forerunners of the Zealots in fighting a holy war against alien rulers.

Magic The manipulation of natural or supernatural forced by spells and rituals for good or harmful ends.

Maimonides, Moses (1135–1204 CE) Jewish philosopher who lived in Spain and later Egypt and attempted a synthesis of Aristotelian and biblical teaching. He listed the Thirteen Principles of belief which have been treated in Judaism as a creed and are found in the Jewish Daily Prayer Book.

Marriage, sacred A religious rite involving real or simulated sexual intercourse which represents the marriage of earth and sky in the fertilization of the soil and the growth of the crops.

Masoretes A group of Jewish scholars from the Babylonian and Palestinian schools who from the seventh to the eleventh centuries CE supplied the text of the Hebrew Bible with vowel points and divided it up into sentences and paragraphs. They also tried to exclude copyists' errors and noted all the variant readings they found.

Meditation Deep and continuous reflection, practised in many religions with a variety of aims, e.g. to attain self-realization or, in theistic religions, to attain union with the divine will. Many religions teach a correct posture, method of breathing, and ordering of thoughts for meditation.

Medium One who is possessed by the spirit of a dead person or a divinity and, losing his or her individual identity, becomes the mouthpiece for the other's utterance.

Mendelssohn, Moses (1729–86 CE) German Jewish rationalist philosopher who taught that the three central propositions of Judaism are: the existence of God; providence; the immortality of the soul. He believed these to be founded on pure reason and to be the basis of all religion. The revelation to the Jews preserves the Jews as an ethnic entity. He translated the Pentateuch into German and encouraged Jews to become more involved in European culture.

Messiah ('anointed one') A Hebrew word referring to the person chosen by God to be king. (1) After the end of the Israelite monarchy it came to refer to a figure who would restore Israel, gathering the tribes together and ushering in the Kingdom of God. Judaism has known several false messiahs (*see* Zevi, Shabbetai). Modern Jews are divided as to whether the messiah is a symbolic or a representative figure and whether the founding of the Jewish state is in any way a prelude to his coming.

Mezuzah ('doorpost') Parchment (often cased) and inscribed with the Shema placed on the door frame of a Jewish house.

Midrash A method of exposition of Hebrew texts designed to reveal the inner meaning of the Torah. Great attention to detail was paid because the texts were believed to be of divine origin. The method was originally oral; the most important midrashim were recorded and written down.

Miracle An event which appears to defy rational explanation and is attributed to divine intervention.

Mishnah A compilation of Jewish oral teachings undertaken by Rabbi Judah HaNasi in around 200 CE. It quickly became second in authority only to the Hebrew Bible and formed the basis of the Talmud. The Mishnah helped Jewish teaching to survive in a period of persecution when the future of the Sanhedrin was in doubt.

Monotheism The belief that there is one supreme God who contains all the attributes and characteristics of divinity.

Moses The father of Judaism who received the Torah from God on Mount Sinai, having led the people of Israel out of captivity in Egypt. The first five books of the Hebrew Bible are traditionally ascribed to him.

Mystic One who seeks direct personal experience of the divine and may use prayer, meditation or various ascetic practices to concentrate the attention.

N

New Year, Jewish *see* Rosh Hashanah.

O

Occult Teachings, arts, and practices that are concerned with what is hidden and mysterious, as with witchcraft, alchemy, and divination.

Old Testament The Hebrew Bible as the first division of the Christian Bible.

Omnipotence All-powerful.

Omniscience All-knowing. Simultaneous knowledge of all things.

Original sin The sin of Adam and Eve, the first human beings, in eating from the forbidden tree in the Garden of Eden, expressing independence from God.

Orthodox Judaism Traditional Judaism which is Talmudic (*see* Talmud) in belief and practice, and is the largest of the modern groupings .

Out-of-body experience Sensation of separation of the self from the body occasionally reported in mystical or drug-induced trance, or as part of a Near-death Experience.

P

Palaeolithic period ('Old Stone Age') The prehistoric age covering from around 2.6 million years ago to c. 10,000 BCE.

Pantheism The belief that all reality is in essence divine.

Passover Seven-day Jewish spring festival marking the deliverance from Egypt (*see* Exodus). Since Talmudic times (*see* Talmud) the festival has begun with a service in the home where unleavened bread, wine, and bitter herbs symbolize the joys and sorrows of the Exodus. There is then a meal and the evening concludes with psalms and hymns which look to God's final redemption of Israel.

Patriarch 'Father-figure'; especially in family and community; in Judaism and Christianity, refers to the founders of the faith such as Abraham, Isaac, and Jacob.

Paul Apostle of Christianity who established new churches throughout Asia Minor and Macedonia. Originally a Pharisee, he was converted by a vision of Christ on the road to Damascus. He wrote several New Testament epistles. Tradition asserts that he was beheaded at Rome under Nero.

Pentateuch *see* Torah (I).

Pentecost Hellenistic name for Jewish harvest festival, fifty-two days after Passover. More usually called *Shavuot* or the Festival of Weeks.

Pharaoh In the Bible, the title of the king of Egypt. The reigning king was identified with the god Horus, and was held to be responsible for the fertility of the land. On death the king became Osiris, his body being mummified and buried in a tomb which from the Third Dynasty to the end of the Middle Period might be a pyramid.

Pharisees Jewish anti-nationalistic party that emerged in the time of the Maccabees. They believed that God was universal and taught the individuality of the soul and the resurrection. They prepared the way for the survival of Judaism after the Fall of Jerusalem in 70 CE.

Philo of Alexandria (c. 25 BCE–40 CE) Jewish philosopher who tried to reconcile Greek philosophy with the Hebrew scriptures. His commentaries used allegorical devices to penetrate the meaning of scripture. He developed the Greek doctrine of the Logos or Word of God into the status of 'a second God'. His speculations were widely studied by the early Christians.

Philosophy of religion The branch of philosophy which investigates religious experience considering its origin, context, and value.

Phylacteries *see* tephillin.

Pilgrimage A journey to a holy place, undertaken as a commemoration of a past event, as a celebration, or as an act of penance (*see also* hajj). The goal might be a natural feature such as a sacred river or mountain, or the location of a miracle, revelation, or theophany, or the tomb of a hero or saint.

Polytheism The belief in and worship of a variety of gods, who rule over various aspects of the world and life.

Prayer The offering of worship, requests, confessions, or other communication to God or gods publicly or privately, with or without words; often a religious obligation.

Prehistoric religion Religions dating from the period before the development of writing.

Priest One authorized to perform priestly functions including mediation between God or gods and humanity, the offerings of sacrifice and the performance of ritual in many religions.

Progressive Judaism Term covering the Liberal and Reform movements which emerged in Judaism in nineteenth-century Europe. Both movements are critical of the Talmudic fundamentalism of Orthodox Judaism and welcome scientific research on the Bible. They also tend to use the vernacular in worship and interpret the dietary laws more liberally than do the Orthodox.

Prophet One who speaks for or as a mouthpiece of God or a god. The Old Testament prophets were social and religious reformers of Israel and Judah and of the people of God in exile. They proclaimed God's prospective judgment of Israel; they recalled the people to obedience to God, some offering a hope of a future vindication.

Prophets, The The second division of the Hebrew Bible, including the histories and the prophetic books.

Psalm A sacred song or poem. The Book of Psalms in the Bible provides the basis for much Jewish and Christian worship.

Purim ('lots') Joyful Jewish festival celebrating the story of Esther, wife of the Persian king Xerxes, who defeated the anti-Jewish plot of the king's steward, Haman.

R

Rabbi ('my master') Jewish religious teacher and interpreter of the Torah. In modern Judaism he or she is a minister to the community, a preacher, and a leader of synagogue worship. Not all Jewish traditions accept female rabbis.

Rabbinic Judaism The religion of the rabbis who – beginning from the second centrury CE – expanded the interpretation of the Talmud and produced authoritative codes of laws, responses, views, and judgments, mostly in the form of correspondence with particular communities.

Relics Bones or remains of saints, venerated and accredited with miraculous powers in many religions.

Religion (from Latin religare, 'to tie something tightly') A system of belief and worship, held by a community who may express its religion through shared myths, doctrines, ethical teachings, rituals, or the remembrance of special experiences.

Renunciation Giving up ownership of material possessions.

Resurrection The raising of all the dead for judgment as taught in Judaism, Christianity, and Islam.

Rites of passage Religious ceremonies which mark the transition from one state of life to another. In many religions these transitional periods are felt to be dangerous and to require spiritual protection. Examples include birth rites, initiation rites, marriage rites, and funeral rites.

Ritual Religious ceremonial performed according to a set pattern of words, movements, and symbolic actions. Rituals may involve the dramatic re-enactment of ancient myths featuring gods and heroes, performed to ensure the welfare of the community.

Rosh Hashanah The Jewish New Year, celebrated as the anniversary of creation. The liturgy is penitential in tone and looks forward to the Kingdom of God and the Messiah. The blowing of the ram's horn, *shofar*, proclaims God as king of the universe.

S

Saadia Ben Joseph (892–940 CE) Head of the Jewish academy at Susa in Babylon. He defended the cause of Rabbinic Judaism against the Karaites and the doctrine of the oneness of God against the Christian Trinity. He was the first Jewish systematic theologian and he believed in the unity and divine origin of both revelation and reason.

Sabbath (Shabbat) Jewish day of worship and rest lasting from Friday sunset to Saturday sunset. The Sabbath is holy because it commemorates God's rest on the seventh day of creation and reminds Jews (2) of the deliverance from Egypt.

Sacrifice The ritual offering of animal or vegetable life to establish communion between humans and a god or gods.

Sadducees Aristocratic Jewish party which emerged in the times of the Maccabees. They rejected the oral law and late doctrines like the Resurrection. They were nationalists and collaborated with the Romans to ensure the survival of the Jewish state. The party collapsed after 70 CE.

Saint Holy person or dead hero of faith who is venerated by believers on earth and held to be a channel of divine blessing.

Salvation In the Bible, deliverance of God's people from their enemies, and especially from sin and its consequences, death and hell, hence also the whole process of forgiveness, new life, and final glorification for the believer.

Sanctuary A place consecrated to a god, a holy place, a place of divine refuge and protection. Also, the holiest part of a sacred place or building. Historically, in some cultures, a holy place where pursued criminals or victims were guaranteed safety.

Sanhedrin Jewish supreme council of seventy which organized religious life during the period of independence following the revolt of the Maccabees. Under Herod the Great the Sanhedrin was divided: the Sadducees

dealt with political matters; the Pharisees concentrated on the interpretation of the Torah. After the Fall of Jerusalem (70 CE) an academic Sanhedrin was organized in Jabneh to reorganize Jewish life.

Satan In the Bible, the personification of evil and identified with the Devil.

Scribes Officials who organized the religious life of the Jewish community after the exile of 586 BCE. They regulated the observance of the Sabbath, communal prayer, and fasting and were the interpreters of the Law. Some copied manuscripts, but this was not necessarily part of their job.

Scripture Writings which are believed to be divinely inspired or especially authoritative within a particular religious community.

Sect A group, usually religious (but it can be political), which has separated itself from an established tradition, claiming to teach and practise a truer form of the faith from which it has separated itself. It is, as such, often highly critical of the wider tradition which it has left.

Sefirot According to the teachings of Jewish Kabbalistic mysticism (*see* Kabbalah), the potencies and attributes by which God acts and makes himself known.

Sephardim One of the two main cultural groups in Judaism which emerged during the Middle Ages. Sephardic Jews lived in Spain and Portugal and their traditions go back to Babylonian Jewry. They developed Ladino as their language.

Seven Precepts of the Sons of Noah The obligations placed on all men and women, regardless of race or faith, according to Jewish teaching. They comprise abstinence from idolatry, blasphemy, incest, murder, theft, the eating of living flesh, and the implementation of justice.

Shabbat *see* **Sabbath**.

Shammai *see* **Hillel**.

Shavuot *see* **Weeks, Pentecost**.

Shekhinah The presence or manifestation of God as described in the Targums and later Jewish writings. It came to refer to the indwelling of God in creation. In Kaballah the Shekhinah is exiled from the eternity of God, Ein Sof, because of human sin and will only be restored at the final redemption.

Shema The Jewish confession of faith, recited in the morning and evening service. 'Shema' is the opening word in Hebrew of the confession: 'Hear, O Israel, the Lord our God, the Lord is One …' Three passages from the Torah confirm that there is one God and that Israel is chosen to witness to him.

Shoah *see* **Holocaust**.

Shulhan Aruch *see* **Karo, Joseph**.

Sin An action which breaks a divine law.

Sin Babylonian moon-god and guardian of the city of Ur.

Sinai, Mount Mountain in the south of the Sinai peninsula where, according to tradition, God revealed himself to Moses and gave him the Ten Commandments.

Sorcerer A practitioner of harmful magic. In indigenous religions sorcerers are sometimes believed to be able to kill others through magic.

Soteriology Teaching about salvation.

Soul (1) The immortal element of an individual man or woman which survives the death of the body in most religious teachings. (2) A human being when regarded as a spiritual being.

Spiritualism Any religious system or practice which has the object of establishing communication with the dead.

Sukkot *see* **Booths**.

Synagogue Jewish meeting place for worship and study. Synagogues grew out of the Torah schools of the scribes during the exile. After the destruction of the temple of Jerusalem (70 CE), synagogues became the centres of Jewish life. They are built to face Jerusalem and contain an Ark (2) in which the scrolls of the law are displayed before a perpetual lamp. Worship in synagogues includes readings from the Torah, psalms, sermons, and communal prayers.

Syncretism The growing together of two or more religions making a new development in religion which contains some of the beliefs and practices of both.

Tabernacles, Festival of *see* **Booths.**

Tallit Jewish prayer-shawl fringed at the four corners and used during morning prayer, Shabbat, and Jewish festivals including Yom Kippur.

Talmud The written interpretation and development of the Hebrew scriptures. It is based on the Mishnah of Judas HaNasi, with the addition of some excluded teachings and commentary recorded from the debates and controversies of the Schools of Babylon on Palestine. There are two versions: the Palestinian, compiled while the Jews were under duress from the Christian Church, and the Babylonian which is more detailed and complete.

Targum A (usually) Aramaic translation of a Hebrew scripture reading. The translator was expected to make a free interpretation. Some of these have become famous in their own right and are used by pious Jews alongside the appointed text.

Tephillin/Tefillin ('phylacteries') Small boxes containing scriptural texts written on parchment. They are worn by Jews (2) on the head and arm during daily prayer.

Temple Building designed for worship of God or gods, usually containing a sanctuary or holy place where sacrifice may be offered.

Temple of Jerusalem/Holy Temple Temple first built by Solomon on a site bequeathed by David. It was divided into the Holy Place and the Holy of Holies where dwelt the presence of Yhwh. This temple was destroyed in 586 BCE. The second temple was dedicated in 515 BCE. It was desecrated by the Hellenistic Seleucid king Antiochus Epiphanes but rededicated by Judas Maccabeus. Rebuilding was begun under Herod the Great in 20 BCE. The temple was virtually completed in 62 CE, but destroyed by Titus in 70 CE.

Tetragrammaton *see* Yhwh.

Theism The belief in one supreme God who is both transcendent and involved in the workings of the universe.

Theocracy ('divine government') Term describing a state which is constituted on the basis of divine law.

Theophany A divine appearance, revelation, or manifestation, usually inducing awe and terror in those who witness it. Examples are the appearance of God to Moses on Mount Sinai amidst thunder, lightning, smoke, and trumpet blasts; the appearance of Krishna in his divine form, 'like a thousand suns', as described in the Bhagavad Gita.

Thirteen Principles Articles of Jewish faith which were formulated by Moses Maimonides in the twelfth century CE. They assert faith in God as creator, as formless unity, First and Last, and only hearer of prayer. They also affirm the words of the prophets, the unchanging nature of Torah, the Creator's knowledge of humanity, the judgment, the coming of the Messiah, and the resurrection of the dead. The Thirteen Principles are found in the Jewish Prayer Book.

Torah (1) The five books of the Law (the Pentateuch) revealed to Moses; the first division of the Hebrew Bible.
(2) 'The teaching', the correct response of Israel to God, outlined in the rules for purity and social justice. It is God's gift to Israel and the way for Israel to fulfil God's call for holiness.
(3) The cosmological principle of order which embraces moral and religious instruction as well as the physical ordering of the universe by God.

Transcendent That which is above or beyond common human experience or knowledge.

U

Underworld The abode of spirits after the death of the body. In many religions the underworld is a shadowy half-real place presided over by a god of death.

W

Wailing Wall *see* **Western Wall.**

Weeks/Shavuot Jewish feast celebrated seven weeks after Passover. It has become associated with the giving of the Ten Commandments on Mount Sinai. Also known as Pentecost.

Western Wall/Wailing Wall/Kotel Site in Jerusalem used by Jews to lament the Fall of Jerusalem and the continuing suffering of the Jews and to pray for restoration. It is believed to be part of the original Herod's Temple, the only part left standing after the destruction of 70 CE. (*See* temple of Jerusalem.)

Witch doctor/Medicine man A healer in indigenous religions. The terms are rarely used today as they are felt to have misleading connotations.

Word of God Christian term for the Bible or part of it.

Worship Reverence or homage to God or a god which may involve prayer, sacrifice, rituals, singing, dancing, or chanting.

Wrath The righteous anger of God against sin.

Writings The third and final division of the Hebrew Bible, comprising the Wisdom literature (such as Job and Proverbs), the Psalms, the later histories, and other material.

Y

Yahweh *see* Yhwh.

YHWH The 'tetragrammaton', the sacred name of the God of Israel which was revealed to Moses. The name means 'I am'. It could not be spoken and the Hebrew '*Adonai*' ('the Lord') was substituted when the scriptures were read aloud. The Masoretes put the vowel points for *Adonai* into the name Yhwh, which gave rise to the malformation 'Jehovah'.

Yom Kippur/Day of Atonement Jewish day of fasting and repentance, the most solemn day of the Jewish year. The liturgy includes a solemn chant, the Kol Nidrei, which challenges Jews who have strayed from religion to return to faith.

Z

Zaddiq/Zadik Jewish teacher in the later Hasidism The zaddiq was *seen* as the perfectly righteous man who was in mystical communion with God. The zaddiq's house became the meeting place for the Hasidim.

Zealots Jewish nationalistic party in Roman times who believed that the Roman presence was a defilement of the land and a flouting of Torah. In 66 CE they revolted. The war which followed led to the destruction of Jerusalem and its Temple in 70 CE. The last stand of the Zealots was at Masada, where 960 of them died in 73 CE.

Zevi, Shabbetai (1628–76 CE) Kabbalistic rabbi from Smyrna who became the centre of a messianic movement which spread throughout the Jewish world (*see* Kabbalah). In 1665 he proclaimed himself messiah. He was later imprisoned and, to the horror of his followers, converted to Islam. There were attempts to argue that the sin of the messiah was a necessary part of redemption, but the movement disintegrated.

Ziggurat Ancient Babylonian temple in the form of a tower rising from a broad base to a narrow top.

Zionism The movement to establish a national and permanent homeland for Jews. In 1897 the First Zionist Congress was organized in Basle by Theodor Herzl in the wake of a wave of European anti-Semitism. Gradually the movement became determined that Palestine was the only realistic place to establish the Jewish state and Jews were encouraged to emigrate and acquire property there.

Zohar Most important writing of the Jewish Kabbalah.

Index

Numbers in **bold type** indicate pages with illustrations.
The Rapid Fact-Finder is not indexed.

Picture Acknowledgments

Dreamstime pp. 18, 31, 43, 46, 97, 105, 120

Illustrated London News pp. 15, 34, 40

Israel Government Tourist Office pp. 81, 95

Israel National Photo Collection pp. 83, 91

Photodisc p. 27

Photolink pp. 85, 86

Tim Dowley Associates pp. 37, 60, 69, 76, 84